# THE MERRITT PARKWAY

# THE MERRITT PARKWAY

BRUCE RADDE

Yale University Press

New Haven & London

Designed by Ken Botnick
Set in Melior type by Tseng Information
Systems, Inc., Durham, NC.
Printed in Canada by Friesen Printers,
Altona, Manitoba.

*Frontispiece*: North Avenue overpass,
Westport, C. 1940. Wood engraving by John
DePol.

Library of Congress Cataloging-in-
Publication Data
Radde, Bruce, 1935–
      The Merritt Parkway / Bruce Radde.
         p.   cm.
      Includes bibliographical references
      and index.
      ISBN 0-300-05379-7 (cloth)
            0-300-06877-8 (pbk.)
      1. Merritt Parkway (Conn.)   I. Title.
TE25.M45R33   1993
388.1′22′097469—dc20          93-9466
                                  CIP

A catalogue record for this book is available from the British Library.

The paper in this book meets the guide-
lines for permanence and durability of the
Committee on Production Guidelines for
Book Longevity of the Council on Library
Resources.

10   9   8   7   6   5   4   3

To my wife, Sally Parker, who has shared my enthusiasm for the Merritt Parkway

# CONTENTS

# PREFACE

The Merritt Parkway. It is probably one of the few highways that inspire reverence and a cultlike devotion among fans and supporters, many of whom use it daily or live near its winding path through Connecticut's Fairfield County. It is known to a much wider audience, however, as one of the earliest successful limited-access[1] regional highways built in the 1930s to cope with the precipitous rise in automobile ownership. Students of urban planning and landscape architecture may not share the same intense feelings as local residents, but they have nonetheless helped enshrine the Merritt as an icon of the automobile age and a model of highway planning. The Merritt Parkway has many notable contemporaries – the Westchester County and Long Island parkway systems leading east and north out of New York City into developing tracts of suburbia, the Pennsylvania Turnpike, the Arroyo Seco (now Pasadena) Freeway, and Hitler's Autobahn in Germany. Yet the Merritt alone among these has inspired genuine affection and achieved the status of a textbook classic.

By the time construction of the second and final section of the Merritt was completed and opened to traffic in 1940, the new road was already acclaimed as special. Not just another highway catering to the burgeoning commuter population trying to get in and out of big cities, it was lauded by design professionals and critics for its excellent engineering, its respect for the natural environment, and its inherent beauty. Others, intrigued that the highway had been built through eight municipal jurisdictions in less than a decade, saw the Merritt as a model of regional planning and cooperation at all levels of government – federal, state, county, and town. And the users of the parkway endorsed its achievement by their sheer numbers: 30,480 cars passed through the Greenwich tolls near the New York–Connecticut line on July 24, 1939, even before the final leg of the 37.5-mile roadway was finished.

The chorus of praise included unexpected voices. Opponents of the project in its early stages often became grudging admirers of the completed work. Although most of the area newspapers were strong supporters from the outset, several, if not openly hostile to the project, had taken editorial and reportorial potshots at the parkway during its difficult planning and construction phases, only to become belated protagonists. No better measure of the near-universal admiration that greeted the Merritt can be found than the enthusiasm expressed by enemy camps within the intelligentsia. As early as 1941, Sigfried Giedion, an International Style activist and technocrat who was the secretary of the Congrès Internationaux d'Architecture Moderne (CIAM), called the Merritt

*Lapham Road overpass, New Canaan, c. 1940 (Department of Transportation, State of Connecticut).*

"a masterpiece of organic layout exemplifying the arrangement of the modern parkway."[2] On the other hand, the humanist scholar and critic Lewis Mumford, long suspicious of what he saw as dubious technological fixes for modern urban ills promoted by the CIAM, was no less lavish in his praise, citing the civilizing effect of the parkway on mechanization.[3]

The finished parkway had its detractors, too, but their voices were lost in the general approbation that both lay and professional commentators heaped on the new road. Ironically, now that the Merritt is entering middle age, a new generation of critics have emerged to advocate radical remodeling of the road or doubling of the traffic lanes from four to eight (which would effectively destroy the parkway as presently known). In this, the Connecticut Department of Transportation has too often seemed a willing accomplice, sacrificing the Merritt's intimate scale and its relationship to nature in favor of an "interstate" image of sweeping interchanges, wide traffic lanes, and broad margins on either side to keep nature at a respectable distance. Recent alterations of the parkway at the interchanges of state highways 8 and 25 in Trumbull and the U.S. Highway 7 interchange – "Super 7" – in Norwalk are totally out of character with the original design. These, along with the Department of Transportation's remarkably insensitive restorations of several aging bridges along the parkway, bring to mind the response that Frank Lloyd Wright made to a local booster who had the temerity to ask Wright what he thought of San Francisco: "Only a city as beautiful as yours could survive what you are doing to it."

The condition in which the parkway will survive is a legitimate concern for devotees of the Merritt – those who can recall leisurely Sunday drives in the 1940s and those who nowadays find this route a saner, more humane alternative to the bleakness and aggressiveness of Interstate 95, the New England Thruway. This book, then, celebrates the Merritt Parkway on its fiftieth anniversary by retelling its history and revealing its beauty, in the hope of enlisting an even wider circle of friends in its preservation.

Many people and institutions have given generously of their time and the materials in their custody to aid in my research. My first and greatest debt, of course, is to the designers and builders of the Merritt Parkway, who have afforded me the enormous pleasure and challenge of documenting the social, political, economic, and design story of their great achievement. I am especially grateful to A. Earl Wood, the engineer who oversaw the original landscaping and roadside development of the parkway and later served as highway commissioner of the State of Connecticut, and to Weld Thayer Chase, the parkway's landscape architect, both of whom fielded questions about the construction of the parkway and graciously made available to me files of newspaper clippings, notes, and correspondence, all of which have immeasurably enriched this text.

I also warmly appreciate the contributions of John R. Smith of Newtown, Connecticut, who provided a copy of his unpublished paper "Merritt Parkway: Anatomy of a Scandal," which helped illuminate a dark chapter in the story, and Professor Pamela Allara of Tufts University, whose unpublished paper "The Bridges of the Merritt: Parkway Theatre" was supplied to me by Mr. Wood. Another one of the pleasures of working on this project has been the remarkable chance encounters with people who have shared with me their stories and insights about the parkway, which I truly appreciate but assume is really a measure of their affection for the Merritt! I hope they will accept this general expression of thanks.

Among the institutions that offered aid and comfort are the Bridgeport Public Library, where David Palmquist, formerly the head of Historical Collections, was especially accommodating. The town libraries of Fairfield, New Canaan, Darien, and Greenwich, as well as the Connecticut State Library in Hartford, opened their files of clippings and other ephemera to me, revealing unexpected treasures of local material on the parkway. In Hartford, Eunice G. DiBella of the Connecticut State Archives took time to secure documents and answer my questions, and Kate Steinway of the Connecticut Historical Society helped turn up several useful items. I have also consulted the local historical societies, whose staffs have been universally helpful. At the New Canaan Historical Society, Marilyn O'Rourke was especially resourceful.

The Connecticut Department of Transportation has provided vintage photos, for the use of which I want to extend my special thanks. All illustrations not otherwise credited, including all color plates, are by the author or are from the author's collection.

For the publication of this book I owe a special debt to Carolyn Battista, a reporter for the *New York Times*, who wrote a piece about my work on the parkway in 1989 while I was a visiting professor at Connecticut College in New London. This was spotted by Judy Metro, senior editor at Yale University Press, who adroitly managed the early phases of getting the manuscript on track. Her colleagues at Yale University Press,

Richard Miller and Ken Botnick, contributed their considerable skills as manuscript editor and graphic designer. My thanks also to Catherine Lynn, who read the manuscript and made a number of useful suggestions.

Finally, while so many have contributed along the way to this book, I must make the time-honored disclaimer of their responsibility for what has been written. For matters of interpretation and errors of fact, I take full responsibility.

Bruce Radde
Fairfield, Connecticut

*Bronx River Parkway, 1922.*

# 1

COPING

WITH

THE

AUTOMOBILE

IN

AMERICA

On June 29, 1938, approximately half the final length of Connecticut's Merritt Parkway — seventeen and a half miles of gleaming white concrete — was officially opened by a motorcade of some forty cars with Governor Wilbur Cross and the aged former congressman Schuyler Merritt, for whom it was named, heading the procession. The day's celebration was marked by the usual political pronouncements and expressions of civic pride. As the motorcade progressed from Norwalk to the New York state line, where the parkway hooked into New York's Hutchinson River Parkway, there were not one but five ceremonial ribbon cuttings — one at each town line and another at the New York–Connecticut line. The big event at the state line, though, never really happened: an impatient and overenthusiastic crowd lunged forward before the yellow ribbon was cut, tearing it to shreds in a scramble for souvenirs. The second half of the parkway was opened incrementally as successive sections were completed over the next two years. The ceremonial opening of the high bridge over the Housatonic River north of Bridgeport on September 2, 1940, completed the thirty-seven-and-a-half-mile traverse of Fairfield County.

So ended nearly two decades of planning and construction of what many still consider the most beautiful limited-access highway ever built.[1] From the perspective of the massive post–World War II highway-building campaign that crisscrossed the nation with superhighways, often virtually destroying the urban cores of major cities, the building of the Merritt Parkway no longer seems the dawning of a glorious new era in transportation as it did in 1940. The official rhetoric and enthusiastic popular acceptance of the parkway, however, were very real. The Merritt was immediately recognized as a special kind of highway whose design emphasized the pleasure of driving without sacrificing such mundane considerations as speed, efficiency, and safety. The populace looked on the parkway not as a utility but literally as a park: rules had to be quickly enacted to restrict picnicking along the roadside, for example.

If the Merritt Parkway embodied qualities rarely associated with its postwar descendants, the interstate highways, it was nonetheless a product of similar forces. Both were conceived as solutions to intolerable traffic congestion and its concomitant, the physically deteriorating highway infrastructure. And once the projects were under way, both became the focus of generous federal largesse — pump-priming efforts designed to fight the Depression in the first instance and to stimulate a stagnant, war-tuned economy in the other.

Opening ceremonies for the Merritt Parkway, June 29, 1938 (Bridgeport Post).

**The Impact of the Automobile**    In Connecticut's Fairfield County, the southwestern portion of the state that abuts New York State and Long Island Sound, the Boston Post Road, which had been designated U.S. Highway 1 under the Federal Highway Act of 1921, had served as the main overland link between New York and Boston and upper New England since colonial times. Even in the eighteenth century it was notorious for its congestion and the poor condition of the roadway. Many travelers used alternate routes to skirt the Connecticut shore by traveling out Long Island and then crossing the sound near its broad upper end to New London or Newport; others avoided the problem entirely by taking a boat between New York and Boston.[2]

In the 1920s most roads outside of cities were still rutted paths, despite the federal highway program. The Post Road was at least paved, although it was only a two-lane highway for much of its length. Beyond serving as the main artery through New England, it also coincided with the main commercial streets running through the centers of the cities and towns along its route, so that through and local traffic were competing for very limited space on the same road. The introduction of cars and of increasingly larger and heavier trucks soon made the situation intolerable. Trucks rumbling along the main streets created massive traffic snarls and extremely hazardous driving conditions during the week. And the institution of the Sunday Drive in the family auto repeated the mess on weekends, even at the height of the Great Depression,

*View of typical rutted, dirt road, c. 1920.*

when such pleasure driving remained one of the few affordable luxuries. The gravity of the situation can be judged from a census of traffic on the Post Road at Greenwich in the late 1920s: some twenty-five thousand vehicles a day were using a route that could comfortably handle perhaps half that many.[3] Obviously something had to be done to siphon off the excess.

Urban traffic jams were certainly not new. The advent of the skyscraper in Chicago in the 1880s had all but insured them as the population density of cities rose with the height of the buildings, which reached twenty stories in Chicago by 1891. But the traffic jam was known even in ancient times. In Pompeii chariots were banned from major pedestrian areas, and when the rule of law failed to cure the traffic problem, blocks of stone were ordered placed in the streets that allowed high-axled commercial carts to pass but blocked youthful lowriders. That the blocks also served as stepping stones for pedestrians to cross the fouled streets was a matter of serendipity.

The difference between Chicago or Pompeii and Fairfield County was precisely the difference between major urban centers and an area then still mainly rural; even today New Yorkers speak more nostalgically than accurately of "going to the country" when traveling to Fairfield's towns. In 1900 the population of the county was only 184,000, and farms and wood lots separated the towns. By the mid-1930s, when the Merritt Parkway was taking shape, the population had reached 350,000 and the Fairfield County Planning Association was projecting that the population would reach 600,000 by 1980.[4] The estimate proved optimistically low: the 1980 census set the figure at 807,143, and by then the quaint and discrete towns along the sound had merged into a virtually unbroken strip of development stretching the length of the county.

It was precisely the bucolic life of Fairfield County that made it so attractive to New Yorkers, and it was the automobile that made "going to the country" possible. Rail transport began to develop in the county by the late 1830s, and by 1849 the New York, New Haven and Hartford Railroad (now the New Haven division of MetroNorth, the commuter railroad) pushed through the county, making access from New York a matter of about an hour's train ride. Although this opened the area for suburban development, the lack of local public transit and good paved roads effectively limited development to two groups: those content to live in the existing towns and cities within walking distance of the train depots, and those whose chauffeured carriages would meet them at the depots and transport them to baronial "country" estates.

The advent of the automobile swept away these limitations. A statistical view of the automobile's phenomenal rise in popularity and availability helps put Fairfield County's and, more narrowly, the Post Road's problem in perspective. In 1895 there were exactly four cars in the entire United States; by 1900 there were eight thousand and by 1940 thirty-two million. Nor has this obsession abated: by 1980 some 175 million cars were registered in the United States, 40 percent of the world's total; the typical household had more cars than children.[5]

The genius of Henry Ford and the American auto industry was to recognize that cars could be made both cheaply and expensively, that they could be both a highly service-able means of transportation and a big-ticket luxury item. Almost from the beginning the car was targeted at all strata of a highly diverse social structure, and this marketing strategy resulted in the nearly universal acceptance of the car as both a necessity and an attribute of modern life. This contrasted with the attitude in Europe, where cars were looked on more as toys, exotic playthings of the wealthy, something to be tinkered with or raced but not to be relied upon for transportation.[6]

The impact of the car on Fairfield County was immediate and profound. The county, especially in areas adjacent to New York State, was becoming essentially suburban in character and wealthy in the extreme, and it remains so today. And though the wealthy might own several cars, even the less affluent could afford a Ford. Thus car ownership was a significant factor in Fairfield's traffic problem from early in the century. And the car, by allowing people to drive to the depot, made the New Haven Railroad a more effective commuter service. But rather than relieve the congestion on the roads this improvement in rail service compounded the traffic problem by encouraging more people to move out of the city. Residents' driving habits, dictated in part by the thinly spread population and the concentration of commercial services along the Post Road, clearly added to the already heavy flow of transient vehicles passing through the county. It became apparent that the problem would only get worse with time.

**Robert Moses's Experiments in New York**          Ironically, the first concrete proposal for relief came not from anyone in Fairfield County or even in Connecticut. In 1923 the Westchester County (New York) Park Commission suggested an extension of the proposed Hutchinson River Parkway into Fairfield County. The proposal technically came from commission officials, but in fact it was part of the grandiose highway scheme of New York's ambitious but little-known director of public works Robert Moses. Moses's elaborate vision spawned a series of limited-access parkways running northward and eastward from New York, expressways to the burgeoning bedroom communities developers were constructing in Westchester County and on Long Island.[7]

Schooled at Yale, Oxford, and Columbia not as an architect or planner but in the humanities and political science, he began to develop his power base modestly enough as the chief of staff of Governor Al Smith's governmental reform commission in 1918. Long before he came to prominence as state commissioner of parks and as master of the revels at New York's 1939 and 1964 world's fairs, and before he gained a reputation for his imperious approach to housing and urban renewal, Moses had begun building the network of roads that remains his most visible contribution to the development of metropolitan New York City.

The first of these were the Northern and Southern State parkways on Long Island, which were proposed in 1924, the year the New York State Council of Parks was created with Moses as its chairman. Construction began in 1926, and by 1929 these two parkways and a string of parks, including Jones Beach with its six miles of waterfront and parking for twenty-three thousand cars, were in place. Through his close ties to Governor Smith, Moses's mark began to appear on parks and roads all over the state, from Fort Niagara in the west to Montauk Point at the tip of Long Island. His efforts were felt in Westchester County with the Taconic, Saw Mill River, and Hutchinson River parkways, all begun in the late 1920s.

Designed as pleasure drives as well as arteries linking Manhattan and the growing suburban belt surrounding the city, these parkways exemplify Moses's major planning contribution, the realization that urban problems had reached such an impasse that only planning at a regional scale could resolve them. These projects also grandly illustrate Moses's personal biases. The Northern and Southern State parkways, for example, were intended, among other things, to provide access to Jones Beach and other projected parks along the south shore of Long Island. But Moses was careful to insure that use of these recreational facilities would be limited to New York's middle-class citizens, not its teeming tenement dwellers: no provision was made for public transit to these beaches, and in fact it was effectively prevented by the deliberate design of low overpasses on the parkways to accommodate passenger cars but not buses. As late as the

1950s Jones Beach remained a de facto segregated facility, "all blonde," as one longtime user remembered it.[8]

The degree of Moses's direct involvement in the design of his various projects is an open question. Robert Caro's exhaustive biography makes it clear that Moses surrounded himself with able designers and engineers, and that his role was often that of an impresario and visionary. His highway schemes were derived from a number of important earlier models upon which he elaborated. The Bronx River Parkway in Westchester County was the first of this new breed of roads and seems to have been the catalyst for much of his work.

Begun in 1907, the Bronx River Parkway took some sixteen years to complete (with time out for World War I). Its modest fifteen miles of four-lane paved roadway twisted through the river valley from the New York Botanical Gardens in the south to the Kensico Reservoir north of White Plains. The general alignment of the road was dictated by the curves and topography of the riverbed, but building it with grade separations for cross roads and limiting access from adjacent properties were purposeful decisions. And although it was designed specifically with the new passenger cars in mind, providing a well-landscaped if narrow strip of park along which pleasure seekers could drive, the original intent of the designers was not to provide a handsome driving environment at all. The Bronx River, especially in its lower reaches, had become an open, running sewer used as a dump by towns and residents along its path. Cleaning up the mess, restoring the river, and, through careful landscaping, masking the often-substandard housing and commercial structures along it were initially promoted by the directors of the Botanical Gardens and the adjacent New York Zoological Society, who feared the effects of the river's pollution on their plants and waterfowl. Consideration of the motoring public was quite coincidental and came only after parkland along the river was already being acquired.

The principal designer and superintendent of construction of the parkway was Gilmore D. Clarke, a landscape architect and engineer.[9] He was ably assisted in the building of the parkway by many designers, most notably Arthur G. Hayden, the structural engineer responsible for the bridges, and Herman W. Merkel, the landscape architect who advised using native plants rather than exotics. Their contributions greatly enhanced the picturesque effect of the road's serpentine course along the river. Charming as it was, the parkway was obsolete by the time it was completed: as Clarke has

candidly pointed out, the road was only forty feet wide (ten feet per lane); it had no median separation and no shoulders for disabled cars, and its curves were both too sharp and inadequately banked. These design flaws can be attributed to the after-the-fact inclusion of this recreational drive in the park strip and to the slow speed, rarely exceeding twenty-five miles per hour, of the early cars for which the road was intended.

Rapid technical developments in cars after 1920, as well as the nearly geometrical expansion in car ownership, quickly brought the problems of the Bronx River Parkway into focus. Moses later corrected some of them – by introducing center dividers, for example – but to this day the drive has a thirty-five-mile-per-hour speed limit, mostly honored in the breach. Nevertheless, Clarke's work was the starting point for most later parkway designs, and some features remain important but too little used in modern freeway layouts. Two sections of the parkway in Scarsdale did have medians as well as (owing to topography) widely separated north and south lanes, which were independently aligned and on different grade levels. The advantages in safety and visual delight offered by widely separating opposing streams of traffic have been realized only occasionally in the Interstate Highway System, even in rural areas where land costs are not a serious consideration.

*Bronx River Parkway, aerial view (Westchester County Park Commission).*

*Bronx River Parkway, 1922.*

**The Legacy of Olmsted & the City Beautiful Movement**     The work of Clarke and his colleagues, though innovative, was not without its own models. Such concepts as grade separations for cross traffic had been pioneered by America's first great landscape architect and urban planner, Frederick Law Olmsted, in his design with Calvert Vaux for New York's Central Park (1856–1876).[10] The curving, rolling carriageways of Central Park were in turn derived from the romantic eighteenth-century English garden tradition, not the broad, uncompromising boulevards of Hausmann's Paris with which they are contemporary. Olmsted had studied English landscape architecture at first hand during his travels there in 1851. In planning Central Park he attempted to bring to the urban context of New York the picturesque vistas that Capability Brown and Humphrey Repton had scattered across the English countryside of the landed gentry. But instead of observing the carefully manicured, "natural" landscape from the terrace of a baronial country house, the patrons of Central Park would commune with Nature from the mobile comfort of a carriage, which allowed them to view his and Nature's handiwork without fear of being sullied by getting too close. Far from the democratic contribution that some have considered Olmsted's work to be, his concept was meant to please a moneyed urban leisure class whose gentility was best served by approaching but never quite touching the carefully contrived, man-made effects of nature with which he filled his numerous – and admittedly handsome – park designs. It is easy to imagine his horror if he saw today the huddled masses attending rock concerts where he had meant for sheep to safely graze.

Olmsted's legacy included contributions to Chicago's Columbian Exposition (1893), where his Central Park innovation of separating carriage and foot traffic with overpasses and underpasses was repeated on a grander scale. There literally tens of thousands of people had to be accommodated on footpaths, on a pioneering elevated railway – the prototype of Chicago's and New York's elevated systems – and on boats fashioned after Venetian gondolas that plied the fair's waterways. The City Beautiful Movement, a product of the 1893 fair, included not only the wave of urban planning that produced such masterpieces as San Francisco's Civic Center complex but also an enthusiasm for park building that spread like a green rash across urban America.[11]

The belief in the salubrious effect parks could have on the urban masses became an article of faith. Planners envisioned cities dotted with wholesome, morally uplifting parks connected by paved carriageways winding through narrow, pastoral strips of parkland. Olmsted himself was responsible for a number of these, most notably Boston's "Emerald Necklace," a series of parks that extended from the Common south through the Fens to Franklin Park. In this 1887 plan, Olmsted threaded the jewels of his park system on a linear greensward of often narrow dimensions that nonetheless managed to keep the urban setting at bay.

These roads had no center median dividers, and intersections were handled by traffic circles derived from English roundabouts, but they showed how "park" and "highway" could be elided to create the "parkway." City Beautiful parkways soon began to appear in Chicago, Kansas City, and a host of other cities, but in all cases, like the Bronx River Parkway, they were conceived as a means of recreational travel or of getting to a recreational area. Robert Moses's contribution to this new genre was simple and ingenious: instead of making the trip an end in itself, an idyllic way to pass a few hours, he turned communing into commuting, a convenient and flexible means of traveling between two points for business, not pleasure.

The parkways Moses built were initially little more than widened versions of Olmsted's Central Park carriageways translated to the countryside. The narrow strips of landscaping along the rights-of-way were simply attenuated parks running for miles through suburbia. The early phases of construction included no median strips to keep opposing traffic streams from head-on collisions, and intersections were often at grade, slowing the flow of parkway traffic while creating hazardous driving conditions. To increase volume *and* safety, Moses's engineers introduced landscaped medians, grade separations, and limited-access features as the projects progressed. A view of the Hutchinson River Parkway, commonly called the "Hutch," shows how these improvements were added after the early sections opened around 1932, when the parkway was pushing toward Connecticut.

Moses has been criticized for his imperious methods, elitist social views, and red-baiting of detractors, but he deserves credit for establishing that urban traffic problems are metropolitan or regional.[12] The vast net of highways he threw around New York also made clear what has become a Murphy's law of traffic planning: traffic volume increases to fill the space available to it. Thus, a new highway built to relieve the pressure on a preexisting, overcrowded road soon fills to capacity without reducing the load on the original route. This became clear in Moses's Triborough Bridge, which was meant to ease traffic from Long Island to Manhattan. It did not, and the Long Island and Westchester parkways seemed to generate thousands of new cars spontaneously as soon as completed. This apparently was a major cause of opposition to building a parkway into Fairfield County. Nonetheless, the situation on the Boston Post Road demanded relief, and with the Hutchinson River Parkway ineluctably approaching the Connecticut line, it became clear to all but the most isolationist observers that New York drivers would soon be flooding the already overtaxed Fairfield County roads. The stage was set for action and reaction.

*Hutchinson River Parkway today.*

*A tapering median strip, White Oak Shade Road overpass, New Canaan (Department of Transportation, State of Connecticut).* **opposite**

# 2

## THE FIGHT OVER A CONNECTICUT PARKWAY

As the traffic problem on the Boston Post Road grew steadily worse, the state responded by widening the road in the countryside – in some areas to three lanes, one of the deadlier transportation inventions of the 1920s. Passage through the main streets of towns along its route, however, remained dangerous bottlenecks. In 1932 accidents on the Post Road in Fairfield County alone claimed ninety-six lives and injured another 2,533 persons, but relief seemed as far away as ever.[1]

The Great Depression should have reduced the crowding, since many people were forced to put their cars up on blocks for the duration of the economic slump, but the opposite was the case. Federal government figures indicate that automobile registrations rose dramatically in Connecticut in the course of the Depression, from 280,307 in 1930 to 418,212 in 1940; for trucks, the figures over the same period more than doubled, from 24,011 to 53,090.[2] Despite the economic hardships, clearly not all the cars were put on blocks. With gasoline selling for under twenty cents a gallon, pleasure driving, especially on Sundays, became one of the most inexpensive family activities available. Commerce between Boston and New York, increasingly diverted from trains to trucks, seemed little affected by the Depression's depredations either. Planners were reported in the press as saying that traffic on the Post Road had reached the saturation point. Obviously something had to be done to unsnarl the traffic.

The proposal by the Westchester County Park Commission in 1923 that a parkway be built to and through Fairfield County was incorporated in the New York Regional Plan, which saw Connecticut as a natural extension of its domain. This proposal for a parkway immediately polarized the citizens of the county. Many of the old Fairfield families, representing venerable New England propertied wealth and Republican virtues, opposed this plan precisely – and quite sensibly – because it would connect with Moses's parkway and bring in hordes of dreaded New Yorkers to pursue their suburban version of the American Dream across the state line into Connecticut. This xenophobia did little to elevate the discussion. For many of these Connecticut natives, the threat of a new highway cutting across their estates and the attendant invasion by outsiders was far greater than the inconvenience of the impacted Post Road.

Few in the opposition expressed their views openly, however. Rather, on June 4, 1924, they formed the Fairfield County Planning Association (FCPA) to serve as their advocate.[3] From the beginning, this powerful but unofficial organization stated that despite its criticism of the New York plan, building a highway across the county was one of its principal objectives. At times, though, the FCPA seemed more dedicated to maintaining the status quo, if not the status quo ante, than to resolving the mess on the Post Road. It drew its membership mainly from the shore communities of the county, since the inland towns were little affected by the traffic concerns that were the initial raison d'être for the FCPA. The organization also advocated from the outset that the county's unique physical and historical qualities be preserved through intelligent application of zoning and planned-development principles. Indeed, as advocate and consultant, the FCPA made significant contributions over the years to the controlled development of the county until it was superseded by the Southwestern Connecticut Planning Association in the 1960s.

It is clear, however, that the FCPA was founded in response to the prospects of a parkway being built in the backyards of an advantaged class; the perceived threat of New Yorkers' immigrating to the country galvanized members of the new organization into action. In its public pronouncements, the FCPA spoke openly of its fear that a highway connecting with New York would inevitably lower property values as "sharpers from out of state" would begin their usual subdivision of the land – thus the need for strict zoning regulations to keep out undesirables.[4] As an FCPA board member, Stamford congressman Schuyler Merritt presumably reflected the organization's thinking when he stated, "A beautiful parkway is not wholly or primarily a means for quick transit, but it should be constructed so as to add beauty to the landscape and, therefore, help to attract desirable residents . . . and add a desirable element to the population."[5] Ironically, studies of the impact of parkways on land values of adjacent properties conducted before World War II proved exactly the opposite: a well-designed, efficient parkway was shown to enhance nearby residential areas precisely because the limited-access feature of such roads prevented the kind of commercial strip development that inevitably came with highways where access is uncontrolled, as exemplified by the Post Road itself.[6]

With influential members like Congressman Merritt, and by means of such tactics as raising the specter of plummeting land values, the FCPA was able to stall a decision on a new road. It also succeeded, by using its strong ties to the state Republican party, in controlling the debate over the kind of highway that might eventually be built. Congressman Merritt again reflected the FCPA's views when he stated that "a real parkway like the Hutchinson Parkway" should be constructed: "But if the result is to be a highway designed and built like a railroad right of way it will desecrate the beautiful country through which it passes and be a damage rather than a benefit to the county."[7] The FCPA campaigned vigorously to insure that any new road would not scar the countryside, demanding that the road follow the topography of the land and make minimum use of cuts and fills, which flatten hills and valleys to create a nearly level road. In fact, their objective was not to build a road for the convenience of commuting newcomers but one for the pleasure and recreation of those already living in the county.

The opposition to cuts and fills was not entirely based on the aesthetic concerns raised by Merritt. The main topographical features of the area – rivers, ridges, and valleys – run mainly north and south while the new road was to run east and west, parallel to Long Island Sound and cutting across these natural features more or less at right angles. In this, the proposed parkway differed radically from Moses's Westchester County roads, which ran mostly north-south following the course of the rivers for which they were named. By keeping cuts and fills to a minimum, the FCPA hoped that the road would have a roller-coaster profile, which in turn would be "an incentive to slow driving" on the road.[8] Their often-expressed fear that the new road would be little more than a speedway to the city was central to shaping the Merritt.

That is not to say that the FCPA was unconcerned about the "beauty" of the finished product, although few of the members believed that that word could properly apply to any superhighway. To minimize damage to the natural setting, they advocated hiring professional landscape architects from the outset to insure that the finished road be returned as nearly as possible to its natural condition after construction ended. They further demanded that far more money be set aside for landscaping than the state had originally budgeted or was accustomed to spending on typical highway projects, which at that time was a pittance. Since the constituency of the FCPA consisted mainly of wealthy property owners and various fox-hunting and other special-interest groups whose lands, well inland from the congested Post Road, would be bisected by the highway, such concerns must be weighed carefully. Their not-in-my-backyard arguments, often couched in terms worthy of latter-day environmentalists, must have sounded somewhat disingenuous even then.[9]

By contrast, people living along the snarled Post Road, as well as local businessmen and those who did commute into New York, supported the Moses plan or something similar as a means of siphoning off some of the Post Road traffic and providing an alternate route. Unlike the landed gentry, these groups, often with disparate interests, failed to organize themselves into a countervailing organization comparable to the FCPA. They certainly had no access to the corridors of power in Hartford, although several newspapers not indebted to the FCPA, such as the *Bridgeport Post* and *Telegraph*, were strongly supportive from about 1923 on.

It was precisely at this point that the state made its first tentative moves to relieve the Post Road problem. In the wake of the initial proposal to extend the Hutchinson River Parkway, John A. MacDonald, the Connecticut state highway commissioner, suggested in 1923 three possible remedies: (1) a new road exclusively for trucks parallel to the Post Road and the New York–New Haven rail line; (2) a new road some twenty miles inland; and (3) further widening of the Post Road with bypasses around major population centers. The first option was realized in the 1950s with the construction of the Connecticut Thruway – Interstate 95 – and the second option became in effect the Merritt Parkway, although it was built on average only about four and a half miles inland. The third option was largely ignored.

### Governor Cross & the Special Fairfield Highway Commission

The reasons for the neglect of MacDonald's proposals may never be established with certainty. Did the FCPA use its strong ties to members of the Republican party elsewhere in the state to forestall action on the proposals, or was the matter one of statewide disinterest in Fairfield County's dire traffic problems? Accounts of the debate in Hartford suggest that representatives from other counties had no sense that Fairfield's needs were any more acute than their own; in any case they believed that the county's traffic problem should not be fixed at the state's expense. (A glance at a map shows how relatively removed the shore points of Fairfield County are from the remainder of the state.)

Ironically, the question of "beauty" became an issue in the debate when legislators from outside the area asked why the rest of the state should pay for "an incentive for slow driving."[10] Some up-staters even suggested that a private toll road might be considered. The tradition of the private road had survived in Connecticut from colonial times until 1905, when the last of these turnpikes was taken over by the recently established State Highway Department (1895). The Highway Department, however, was not about to relinquish its monopoly on highway building.

The impasse between the needs of Fairfield County and the disinclination of the rest of the state to provide funds further delayed plans for the proposed parkway. Yet this small county contained a disproportionate part of the state's population, including Bridgeport, then the third-largest city. This is not to say, however, that the project had gone entirely unnoticed in Hartford. In 1925, a date some take to be the official beginning of the Merritt Parkway, the legislature allocated fifteen thousand dollars for a Highway Department survey of the county's highway needs. In 1927 legislative approval was given in principle to a measure providing for a new trunk highway – not a parkway – running westerly from Stratford in the east to the New York state line in the Glenville section of Greenwich.[11] No money was appropriated for its construction; instead, funds were to come from regular Highway Department allocations.

It was also in 1927 that the Fairfield County Republican organization first suggested that the new road should be called the "Merritt Boulevard" in recognition of the years of service that the Republican congressman Schuyler Merritt had given to the county. Merritt graciously accepted the nomination, but suggested the use of *parkway* instead of *boulevard,* pointing out the inappropriateness of a term derived from military fortifications for so idyllic a route.

By 1931 a legislative package had been passed directing the highway commissioner to lay out and develop the "Merritt Highway." Another act from the same session called for the governor, Wilbur Cross, to establish a locally based Merritt Highway Commission to build and maintain the road. This provision was gutted by the Republican attorney general's twisted legal interpretation that the commission would be empowered only *after* the new road was completed, a reading clearly not intended by the legislature. Establishing this independent commission had been more than a goodwill gesture extending home rule to the new highway; it also was intended to assuage local resistance to the new road which had resulted from the efforts of several town planning boards to involve themselves in the project. By transferring control to a regional board made up of leaders of the towns through which the road was to run, traditional state authority was passed to a county, not to the towns. State Highway Commissioner MacDonald clearly saw a parallel regional highway commission as a threat to his empire, but under the attorney general's ruling, which he had sought, he retained full power and authority over the planning and construction of the highway. This left the nine new commissioners, including Merritt, with little to do but sit and wait for the completion of the project. While waiting they took what action they could, criticizing MacDonald's efforts and otherwise trying to wrest control of the project from the embattled state highway commissioner.

Yet another 1931 act appropriated $1 million for right-of-way acquisition and construction, the first substantive support the project had received from the state. But as the Depression deepened, Hartford's interest in the Merritt Parkway receded. MacDonald, however, moved ahead on the project quietly and slowly. He had acquired the first parcels of right-of-way as early as 1931, although the first construction contract was not awarded until June 1934, with effective construction put off until the spring of 1935. By then unemployment in Connecticut, as everywhere, was rampant, and pressure was building for government intervention. The construction industry and allied industries had been especially paralyzed by the collapse, and the prospect of lucrative contracts to build the new road brought the construction companies and their unemployed workers solidly into the fold of parkway supporters.

Meanwhile, resistance to the Merritt project was encountered in several town councils along the proposed route. Rumors circulated that moneyed interests were actively trying to stop the parkway before construction had even started. Some cynically held that the New Haven Railroad was lobbying against it to keep the Post Road dangerously entangled for the good of the railroad's commuter business; others circulated stories about the landed gentry's contributing political campaign funds with the prior agreement that candidates would vote against any parkway measure.[12] To counter such opposition and get the project off dead center, State Senator E. Gaynor Brennan, Republican of Stamford and a supporter of the parkway, proposed empowering the titular Merritt Highway Commission immediately, increasing its membership from nine to fifteen, and expanding the scope of its responsibilities. Brennan suggested that his proposal would bring the people of Fairfield together behind the project if they had substantial control of its development, adding, "Let County folk develop the Parkway, it's theirs."[13] The measure never reached the floor of the legislature.

**Financing the Parkway**    In the chemistry of the political process all of these factors came together or evaporated, as the case may be, when Governor Cross made the issue moot by signing a bill on June 13, 1935, that insured the financing of the project and finally extended some real power – financial power – to the Merritt Highway Commissioners. The original $1 million allotment of 1931 had not lasted long, going entirely for land acquisition in Greenwich, where property values were greatest. MacDonald estimated that the total cost of the highway would amount to a then-staggering $20 million.[14] A number of efforts to guarantee financing the project for the duration expired quietly in the state legislature. For example, Assemblyman J. Kenneth Bradley, Republican of Westport, proposed a measure in 1933 to empower an expanded and strengthened Merritt Highway Commission to sell up to $20 million in bonds for construction and right-of-way costs. The Bradley bill was also stillborn at the end of the legislative session, however, and under state law only the legislature had the authority to bond the state or a county.

Governor Cross claimed to support construction of the Merritt, but he wanted it built on the cheap. He resisted all efforts to have him call a special session of the state assembly in 1934 to resolve the legislative blockade, even though selling state bonds would have made the project eligible for federal economic recovery grants. (His resistance seems to have been based on his canny understanding that a special session, once called, might pursue any mischief it wished, a chance he was not prepared to take.) Meanwhile, not a shovel of dirt had yet been turned on the site of the Merritt Parkway.[15]

The 1935 legislative session was moving rapidly toward adjournment when Bradley, now a state senator, maneuvered a scaled-down version of his earlier bill, calling for the sale of only $15 million in bonds, into a position for legislative review. He was aided in this effort by a fellow Fairfielder, Senator Charles Rumpf of Darien, chairman of the Senate Roads, Rivers and Bridges Committee. Simultaneously he engineered support outside the legislative halls, most notably the friendly intervention of Schuyler Merritt with the relief agencies in Washington, in a desperate attempt to force action in the senate. His obdurate Republican colleagues were again prepared to reject the parkway financing plan as an extravagance when Bradley announced in the midst of the floor debate that a federal pump-priming grant of $400,000 had just been made available, with the promise of a further grant of $6.25 million and a federal loan of $8.5 million at a modest 3 percent interest rate.[16]

These moneys, Bradley stated, would insure construction jobs for two thousand workers on relief. He added, coincidentally, that the federal funds were conditional upon the state providing a roughly equal share. This infusion of good old-fashioned federal money caused the state's rights idealism of the state assembly to vanish faster than the legislators could say "creeping socialism." The measure authorizing Fairfield County to sell $15 million in state bonds was passed quickly and unanimously in both houses and sent to the governor.[17] His signature put the act into effect immediately under one of the provisions of the bill. For once everyone seemed satisfied: workers and construction companies could look forward to an influx of federal money; Fairfield County would finally see some real progress toward relieving the congestion on the Post Road; and the governor could face his up-state constituency – he was from New Haven – without being accused of favoring one section of the state at the expense of the remainder. At the signing ceremony Cross said, "The time is particularly opportune for the immediate completion of this project, particularly since . . . the Federal government is ready to advance 45 per cent of the cost as a grant under the new Federal program."[18] He then presented the pen used in the signing to Senator Bradley.

The euphoria over the bill's passage was premature, however. The federal funding was to prove illusive. The promised fast-track construction was stalled, to the frustration of contractors and workers, by planning delays and bureaucratic procedures. And before long the discovery of massive and seamy graft led many to wonder if the parkway would ever be finished at all.

# 3

## MAPPING THE ROUTE, UNCOVERING THE CORRUPTION

*Jess Benton editorial cartoon, "Hidden Names Cloud Parkway Plunder,"* Bridgeport Sunday Herald, *December 26, 1937 (New Canaan Historical Society).*

Many people were caught off guard in 1935 by the sudden turn of events in Hartford when the legislature approved Senator Bradley's proposal for funding the Merritt Parkway. They were also surprised by the progress in acquiring the land for the right of way that John MacDonald and his staff at the state highway commission had already made over the previous years, when they only had available the limited funds drawn from the regular Highway Department budget. Considering the years of acrimonious debate, the efforts – real or imagined – to sabotage the project, the conflicting interests of various parties, and the host of other problems that beset the parkway in its period of gestation, the actual construction, once begun and properly funded, moved ahead amazingly rapidly. Rough grading and construction began in the spring of 1935, almost as if in anticipation of Bradley's June legislative coup. The first seventeen miles of the road were opened to traffic on June 29, 1938, the remainder incrementally as finished. The parkway was completed on September 2, 1940, with the opening of the Housatonic River bridge in Stratford, the most ambitious single structure of the project. Thus, the construction phase took only a bit over five years, using technology far more primitive than the massive earth moving-equipment that is now routine in such work: much of the work was done by hand, and horse-drawn equipment was still common.

The fifteen thousand dollars appropriated by the legislature in 1925 to do a feasibility study for a road paralleling the Post Road was used by Commissioner MacDonald to begin mapping a tentative route through the county. MacDonald was apparently not a trained civil engineer but had worked his way through the ranks to become head of the Highway Department, a post he assumed in 1922. He applied surprisingly up-to-date methods in plotting the future route, most notably aerial surveillance, a technique introduced in the then recently concluded world war. With such techniques he was able to project a route that wound a path through the area's complex geography while taking advantage of open space to avoid the added cost of acquiring heavily developed land, especially the manorial country houses in the Greenwich area. But even as the survey proceeded, MacDonald's commitment to the project was flagging: early in 1929 he advocated abandoning the Merritt on the grounds that the Post Road would be adequate until "at least 1936."[1]

MacDonald and his engineers established a uniform right-of-way width of three hundred feet running the length of the projected road. Some additional small parcels of land that would have been cut off from adjacent surface streets were also acquired, extending out from the three-hundred-foot strip. Given these vagaries of geography and property lines, the route from the New York line to the Housatonic River is remarkably direct. Driving the finished parkway gives a much greater impression of numerous sweeping curves than is actually the case; on the other hand, the finished road is also far from the "railroad right of way" that Schuyler Merritt had warned against. In fact, the road as built is 84 percent trangent – the engineer's term for a straight alignment – and only 16 percent curves. The Westchester County parkways, by contrast, are laid out in twisting routes with tight curves because they hug the streams for which they were named. In this the Merritt marks an important improvement over its models. On the other hand, the maximum grade in crossing the various ridges is an 8 percent rise – eight feet of elevation per one hundred feet of road – with an average grade of only 4 percent. (The slope of a typical Manhattan sidewalk, from building line to curb, is about 2 percent.) These relatively steep grades were unavoidable without resort to tunnels, which were not used because of added costs, or extreme cuts and fills, which would have badly scarred the landscape. Inevitably, some persistent critics referred to the result as "an engineer's roller coaster."[2]

The precise considerations MacDonald brought to bear and the exact methods he used to map the parkway's route can only be inferred from what was actually built. From the outset, the commissioner veiled his activities in great secrecy, keeping details of the proposed route from all but his closest associates in the Highway Department. He especially excluded the Merritt Highway Commission, which had been neutralized in any event by the ruling that its mandate would not become effective until the new road was completed: the 1935 legislation had allowed the commission to assume a bonded debt but had not reversed the attorney general's crippling ruling.

The route eventually established was the product of many conflicting interests. Ultimately, it was MacDonald who was mainly responsible for site selection, but the legislature clearly had a stake in the outcome. The 1931 bill that mandated construction of a road parallel to the Post Road had specifically called for a parkway, not a conventional highway. It also indicated that the route should bend south toward the sound in Trumbull to connect with the Post Road at or near the Washington Street bridge over the Housatonic River, which joins Stratford and Milford. The present high bridge over the Housatonic was an afterthought that itself required special legislative authorization for realignment of the parkway well into the construction phase.

The Merritt Parkway Commission, although officially disenfranchised, continued efforts to effect changes in the route through its contacts in Hartford. Several commissioners were members of the legislature, but because MacDonald sat on the commission ex officio, he was aware of their efforts and could parry them. Meanwhile, the Fairfield County Planning Association had hired a full-time planning engineer, Joseph T. Woodruff, and armed with various studies he and his staff had made, the FCPA continued its own efforts to influence the project through lobbying and public relations. Then there were the conflicting interests of the towns through which the road was to pass, which the emasculated Merritt Highway Commission was supposed to resolve but could not, and the rearguard resistance of individual property owners and neighborhood associations. Some determinants were entirely out of Connecticut's control. If the Merritt were to have any utility, it had to tie into the Hutchinson River Parkway, whose route lay closer to Long Island Sound than planners and property owners in Greenwich wanted. Under the circumstances, it is not surprising that MacDonald held his cards so close to the vest, although this very habit of secrecy finally contributed to his downfall.

Not everyone remained in the dark, although another of MacDonald's decisions kept the informed circle as tight as possible. Virtually all of the planning, design, and construction supervision was done within the Highway Department by MacDonald's trusted lieutenants. None of the engineering was farmed out, nor were consultants hired for any phase of the project. By contrast, Robert Moses routinely hired out such work — Gilmore Clarke's firm, for example, worked closely with Moses for over three decades on various projects including the 1964 World's Fair. Beyond secrecy and aggrandizement of personal power, MacDonald's in-house approach had the advantage of bringing the talents of a tight-knit group of professionals to bear on the problem in a familiar environment with a minimum of barriers to communication. An example of the thoroughness of this vertical organization is seen in the contributions of staff landscape personnel. Once the route for a given section was established, but before construction began, landscape designers would walk the route and carefully mark trees near the roadway and shoulders that were to be saved in order to minimize the environmental impact. To what degree this policy contributed to the first-rate success the Merritt proved to be can only be speculated upon, but along with the brilliant staff he assembled, the decision to keep the design of the parkway in-house may well represent one of MacDonald's most important contributions to the project.

Still, the commissioner's habit of secrecy undoubtedly contributed to major problems and created unnecessary friction. Several weeks before the approval of the landmark funding bill, for example, and with actual construction on the parkway moving ahead at both the Greenwich and Stratford ends, the *Bridgeport Post* discovered with some alarm that a map of the proposed route had yet to be published. And MacDonald declined to provide one. Unhappily, he also declined to give one to State Senator Charles Rumpf, Republican of Darien, who chaired the Senate Committee on Roads, Bridges, and Rivers. This led directly to a legislative demand that MacDonald make a map of the route public forthwith. A schematic map first appeared in the *Post* on May 20, 1935, and in July, after the bond issue had been resolved, MacDonald met with Rumpf's committee to provide a more detailed map of the layout.

The funding legislation had named Rumpf, a civil engineer by training, to be a kind of supervising engineer for the Merritt project, and had designated Kenneth Bradley,

*First map of the proposed Merritt Parkway route (Bridgeport Post, May 20, 1935).*

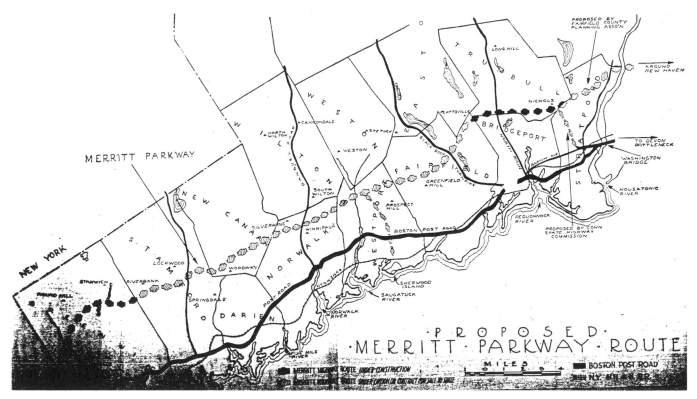

the Westport senator who had carried the bill, as its special attorney. These moves seem to have intimidated the highway commissioner into mending his ways. Discovery at the same time by Woodruff that the construction was proceeding with massive cuts and fills to create a "railroad right-of-way" rather than the mandated parkway sympathetic to the natural landscape also contributed to the trimming of MacDonald's authority.[3] It was at this time that A. Earl Wood was reassigned from the Highway Department's landscape division as full-time engineer for landscaping and roadside development on the Merritt project, a post he held until the completion of the parkway.

From our present perspective, conditioned by requirements for environmental impact reports and other layers of governmental and citizen overview for even quite minor undertakings, it is difficult to imagine how so extensive a project could have reached such an advanced stage without serious public scrutiny. Even the WPA, the dispensing arm of federal support, was anxious to approve the funds without reviewing a single document. Leslie A. Hoffman, the resident WPA engineer for Connecticut, admitted that neither plans nor an official application for aid had been submitted to his office as late as July 5, 1935, although the promise of federal aid had already been made back in May.[4]

Equally baffling are MacDonald's motives for shrouding the exact route in secrecy. He probably hoped to save the state money by preventing the speculative buying that seems inevitably to accompany any governmental land acquisition project. In fact, he had as many as eight alternate routes plotted out, but which one was the actual path could hardly be guessed. Ironically, the very secrecy of his methods triggered serious land speculation. It also fostered the graft that ultimately ended his career.

**Leroy Kemp & the Great Land Swindle**          MacDonald's domain included the Bureau of Rights-of-Way and Highway Boundaries, the agency that normally would have overseen title searches and land acquisition through the state's right of eminent domain. Instead, he bypassed this established unit in favor of a special ad hoc state purchasing agent. Once again, it is unclear whether the idea for the special purchasing agent was MacDonald's or someone else's. Two things are clear, however. First, the commissioner stated that he favored negotiated purchases of land over condemnation proceedings. He claimed that condemnation would be more costly and time-consuming, although as it turned out the negotiated purchases were hardly less expensive. Second, Republican party regulars in Hartford and in Fairfield County not only favored the special-agent approach, presumably as a way of retaining greater control of the process than would be possible if it were turned over to the bureaucracy, but they also had a candidate for the job. G. Leroy Kemp, a former Republican assemblyman and the owner of a Darien-based real estate brokerage, was named to the post of independent procurer by MacDonald in 1932. He was given responsibility for acquiring some twenty-six hundred acres of land needed for the right-of-way at a modest salary of fifteen dollars per diem. Kemp set out to amend his pay by working out fifty-fifty kickback deals with two other agreeable brokers, Thomas N. Cooke, a Greenwich realtor, and Samuel Silberman, a Stamford agent, whose flexible ethical standards matched his own.

MacDonald may have agreed with the Kemp appointment because he needed someone familiar with the complexities and current values of Fairfield County real estate. He could hardly have *not* hired him, however, since Kemp's roster of supporters included Harry E. Mackenzie, president of the Fairfield County Republican party, Republican State Central Committeeman Charles E. Williamson, Republican National Committeeman Samuel F. Pryor, Jr., and a host of elected officials from Fairfield County. MacDonald was himself a solid Republican and was beholden to the party for retaining his position when Democratic governor Wilbur Cross took office in 1930. Certainly he had no reason, with such impressive support, to suspect that Kemp's job skills included a penchant for graft.

Nor, apparently, was he ever aware of Kemp's modus operandi.[5] Kemp would inform his friends in the real estate business what parcels of land were needed, and they would then approach the owners, offering their services to negotiate the selling price with the state. Since MacDonald had kept the exact route a secret, the first news that people generally got was when the realtors contacted them. The secrecy also had the added charm of keeping other, nonconspiratorial realtors out of the game, since they would have no way of determining which owners to approach. For this privileged information the contact realtors agreed to split their fees with Kemp, who insured that their own percentage commissions remained sufficiently attractive by the simple expedient of offering selected landowners, some of whom were FCPA or Republican party members (or both), sweetened deals they could hardly resist.

In theory, landowners could have dealt directly with the state, bypassing a broker and thus saving his commission. In fact, however, few did. The negotiations and red tape could eat up time and money, and, as a grand jury later reported, Kemp proved to be an elusive purchasing agent, preferring to work through his own brokers. Once a figure had been agreed upon, Kemp would report to his immediate supervisor, War-ren M. Creamer, the state engineer in charge of design and construction for the Merritt project. Creamer, in turn, would approve or modify the recommendation before sending it to MacDonald for his review, at which point a voucher would go to the state comp-troller, who would issue the check. Creamer's lauded expertise as an engineer did not extend to Fairfield County real estate deals, and MacDonald only occasionally rejected the recommendations that came to his desk, so that Kemp and his friends effectively had a free hand in indulging their cupidity.

The prices Kemp's agents offered certainly helped to speed the land acquisition process, thus proving MacDonald partly right in his assumption that negotiated deals would go faster than condemnation proceedings. On the other hand, the exorbitant prices that were paid inflated the overall cost of the parkway, though by how much will never be known. Too few eminent domain suits against recalcitrant landowners were prosecuted to get a fair estimate of what court awards might have been had more suits been brought. Kemp's prices routinely exceeded the assessed value of land by fac-tors of two to five and sometimes by ten or more. For example, a tiny parcel of land in Greenwich measuring 0.216 acres and assessed at seventy dollars fetched one thousand dollars.[6]

Granted that the assessed value of a property rarely matches its fair-market value, the prices offered by Kemp could still be breathtaking, especially in the depressed real estate market of the Thirties. But as his deals progressed, the unfair differentials in what was being paid began to be rumored. Inevitably, people grew suspicious even if Creamer and MacDonald did not. Again in Greenwich, two parcels, one of about ten and a half acres valued at $18,051, the other of about fifteen acres and, at $7,458, less than half the value of the first, were bought by the state for $32,000 and an astonish-ing $93,000, respectively. In some cases it is not clear whether it was Kemp's greed, Yankee shrewdness on the sellers' part, or plain bureaucratic bungling that triumphed. The Nellie Joyce caper, yet again in Greenwich, was characterized by a grand jury as an "example of reprehensible practices."[7] Kemp originally got the needed portion of the property for $96,621, plus another $17,000 for the state to move Joyce's house elsewhere on the property and to provide – and here was the bureaucratic blunder – *direct* parkway access to the new location. With many acres of undeveloped land still in her holdings, Joyce threatened to build a subdivision with its own access to the limited-access parkway, and the state's only recourse was to buy the moved house and disputed property again, but this time for $148,000. (The State ultimately recouped some of the excessive payment in the courts.)

Kemp's brazenness could border on the churlish. Through his co-conspirator Silberman he sold twenty-five acres of his own land in Westport, a tract called Westport Estates, Inc., which the town of Westport valued at $13,618. Kemp hired independent appraisers (a common practice for him) but rejected their figure as too low. He then appointed a second appraisal committee and, concealing the initial report, accepted their recommendation of $183,000 – some four times the original appraisal and more than ten times the assessed value. He then split the brokerage fee with Silberman.[8]

By 1937, Kemp's scam began to unravel. Creamer now suspected that some awards were excessive. Some watershed, for example, was purchased from the Greenwich Water Company by which Clarence G. Willard of New Haven, secretary of the Republican State Central Committee, was paid $3,700 out of the brokerage commission for what the grand jury called "friendly services and influence in expediting the sale."[9] Creamer refused to approve the deal and suggested similar action to MacDonald, who promptly certified the sale price to the comptroller. This forced Creamer to become even more vigilant and eventually turned him into a whistle-blower.

At about the same time, Governor Cross's long battle with the Republican-dominated senate (the assembly had passed to Democratic control in 1932) to approve reform legislation giving effective control of budget development and accountability to the executive began to bear fruit. Leaks about irregularities in land acquisition, not just on the Merritt project, reached the governor's office, and Cross quietly put some trusted aides to work investigating the allegations.

Attorney General Edward Daly uncovered enough evidence by April 1937 to convince Cross that the Highway Department was rife with dubious deals. Further probing by Loren W. Willis, the state's attorney for Fairfield County, led to the convening of a special grand jury on January 8, 1938. But before Cross could act, investigative reporters from the *Bridgeport Post* broke the story on December 17, and soon all the papers of Fairfield County were filled with the latest titillating details of what the leftist *Bridge-*

*port Sunday Herald* headlined a "Get Rich Quick Plot to Gouge State." [10] Since property assessments and real estate sales are a matter of public record, the newspapers soon began naming those who seemed to profit excessively and those whose purchases of property and resale to the state bore an uncanny resemblance to insider trading.

Kemp, meanwhile, attempted a classic coverup, destroying or altering records and colluding with his co-conspirators on their projected testimony. When the press tried to question him, he referred them to his boss, MacDonald, who responded with a stony "No comment." The Democrats smiled as Republican damage controllers scrambled to isolate Kemp from the shabby involvement of high party officials. The Bridgeport Communist party engaged in righteous finger pointing, charging that "some of our best citizens, who are the first to complain of the costs of relief, are undoubtedly involved in this violation of the public trust." [11] Ultimately, Kemp alone stood trial for the misdeeds. The proceedings lasted two weeks, and the press reported that Kemp was "near tears as trial ends." [12] The jury took only two and a half hours to convict him, and the judge sentenced him to three to seven years in prison, not only for the documented $43,000 he had extracted from the citizens of Connecticut over the previous five years, but also for compromising the public trust. Cooke and Silberman got off with unusually light sentences in exchange for guilty pleas – a mere five-hundred-dollar fine. But as the judge noted, theirs was not the position of public servant.

The effects of the Kemp disclosures were immediate and highly visible. The prices paid for additional Merritt Parkway land acquisitions went down sharply. And responding to the grand jury's findings that John MacDonald, though not criminally culpable, had so badly mismanaged the Highway Department that he should be replaced, Governor Cross asked for and received MacDonald's resignation on April 30, 1938.

# 4

## DESIGNING & BUILDING THE MERRITT PARKWAY

The cloak of secrecy in which John MacDonald wrapped his plans for the Merritt Parkway makes it difficult to know his original intentions and hence how much of the design can be attributed to him. It is fairly clear, however, that a very different road would have emerged had he retained design control throughout the project. What can be pieced together from contemporary news accounts makes apparent that he did not take seriously the insistence of the FCPA and Schuyler Merritt that the road should enhance the beauty of Fairfield County, not detract from it. His would have been a no-nonsense highway cutting a swathe across the landscape, an engineer's solution to a nagging problem, not a landscape architect's attempt to integrate a modern limited-access highway into a mostly rural setting of quiet charm and natural beauty.

MacDonald's utilitarian approach is corroborated by the discovery in mid-1935 by Joseph Woodruff, of the Fairfield County Planning Association, that work under way in Greenwich and Stratford ignored official guidelines for scenic preservation. His design would have flattened and straightened the route, arguably making it faster and safer, but also eliminating those features that set the Merritt apart from comparable highways of the period.

Aside from its grades and curves, the present parkway differs from what a Mac-Donald parkway would have been in several other respects. Initially, MacDonald had planned a single roadbed forty feet wide and without a median divider. By late July 1935 he was proposing two strips, each twenty-seven feet wide and separated by a median of forty-one feet. In December the commissioner and the Merritt Highway Commission agreed upon two twenty-foot lanes with a divider of unspecified width, presumably to be worked out by MacDonald and his engineers. The final design was closer to the July 1935 plan: two strips, each measuring twenty-six feet from curb to curb, separated by a landscaped median with a normal (but varying) width of twenty-two feet four inches.

As late as February 1936, however, this plan seemed far from final in the mind of the chief field engineer, Warren Creamer. Following a presentation to the Connecticut Society of Civil Engineers, Creamer responded to a question about the uniform width of the median: "I don't know [if it will be uniform]. The Commissioner [MacDonald] hasn't given a definite opinion on that yet. It may be varied."[1] These vastly different proposals represented only a few of the options considered. The Biennial Report of the Highway Commissioner for 1940 noted without elaboration that the final parkway design "was decided upon after endless studies of the subject."[2]

*Rippowam River bridge, c. 1938 (Department of Transportation, State of Connecticut).*

One design feature remained constant from the beginning. The 300-foot right-of-way was divided down the middle into two 150-foot strips with construction assigned to the northern strip. The southern 150 feet was officially reserved for possible future expansion of the parkway, a proposal that remained dormant until the 1980s, when rush hour congestion on the Merritt sparked controversial renewal of interest in the original scheme. From the outset, unofficial proposals advocated a variety of uses for the reserved strip. One plan called for building a parallel route for trucks and commercial vehicles; others ranged from leaving it as a permanent greenbelt or buffer to building the four-lane parkway down the center of the right-of-way with a seventy-five-foot greenbelt on either side. Some proposed that a network of bridle paths be constructed on it, and Fairfield County Sheriff Thomas Reilly suggested a bicycle path to keep cyclists off the parkway.[3] In 1993, the southern strip remains undeveloped and contributes to the parkway's idyllic corridor.

**Engineering the Parkway**        If John MacDonald ultimately lost control of the Merritt project, his early influence strongly affected the final design. Authority began to slip through his fingers as a result of the FCPA's summer of discontent in 1935, well before Kemp's perfidy brought him down; but by that time many basic design concepts, presumably MacDonald's, had informed the total project.

Chief among these was a cost-cutting idea that may have reflected the financial realities of the Great Depression and MacDonald's penchant for saving any dollar he could. A significant but undetermined amount was saved by reducing the landscaped median strip from twenty-one feet to a mere sixteen-inches of concrete curb at overpasses and underpasses, thus minimizing the spans of the bridges and so their cost. This resulted in what later came to be called the "pinched bridges," much criticized for causing a convergence of opposing traffic at each bridge. Safety was similarly compromised by a number of the overpasses, which were double-arched designs with substantial concrete supports in the center. This meant that the inner lanes were brought into uncomfortably close proximity with either immovable objects or oncoming vehicles. The narrowing of the median strip also forced drivers to steer toward impending danger as they approached it, setting up a classic approach-avoidance conflict. Once these bridges were constructed, of course, the problem was literally cast in concrete and could be altered

*A pinched bridge, Route 137 overpass, Stamford, c. 1940 (Department of Transportation, State of Connecticut).*

only at enormous cost. Frequent users of the Merritt soon accept this as one of its design quirks; for the novice, especially when driving at night, it can be quite exhilarating to approach what seem to be converging headlights. (The addition of corrugated steel barriers to the median in recent years has mitigated this problem if not enhanced the visual effect of the parkway.)

Another product of cost containment is the unusually tight and sometimes unbanked curving entrance and exit ramps. Many of the ramps are double-loaded; that is, entering and exiting traffic share lanes divided only by a stripe of yellow paint. The money saved in additional grading, pavement, and guardrails is offset by the fact that most ramps cannot be negotiated safely at speeds much above twenty-five miles per hour. Nor, for similar reasons, did the original layout include long acceleration and deceleration lanes: most drivers soon learn the fine art of braking quickly at the last moment and heading into the exit at nearly full parkway speed. Entering the crowded parkway without an acceleration lane can be an even more exacting test of a driver's skill and courage: since most entrance lanes now are equipped with stop signs, a driver must merge with speeding traffic from a dead stop.

*A tapering median strip, White Oak Shade Road overpass, New Canaan (Department of Transportation, State of Connecticut).*

*Double-loaded entrance ramps, Black Rock Turnpike interchange, Fairfield, c. 1940 (Department of Transportation, State of Connecticut).*

The Merritt Parkway shared these features with various of Robert Moses's parkway designs in Westchester County and elsewhere in Greater New York. It was from these, most notably the Hutchinson River Parkway to which the Merritt was to connect, that MacDonald and his staff no doubt took their cues. The dangers to navigation that these features created were recognized before construction began on some of the later phases of the work and were corrected; where possible, ramps were made single-loaded, curves were made more generous or even eliminated as in the Main Street interchange in Trumbull, and the pinched bridges were abandoned. In those sections of the roadway first completed, however, these remain as long shadows of MacDonald's tenure as highway commissioner.

**The New Design Team**            Trimming MacDonald's authority in 1935 meant that the shaping of the road became a more broadly shared responsibility. Warren Creamer remained the chief project engineer in the field, but the legislative appointment of Senator Charles Rumpf as oversight engineer created another layer of authority. At the same time, another specialist was added to the design and engineering team when MacDonald transferred A. Earl Wood from the general landscaping division of the Highway Department to a full-time position in charge of landscaping and roadside development for the Merritt. This move was apparently intended to insure the beautification of the finished road in a way more compatible with FCPA wishes.

MacDonald's diminished role did not so much create a vacuum as increase the responsibilities of the staff. In addition to Creamer and Wood, the principal design engineers were John Smith and Leslie Sumner, who laid out the roadway and did the structural engineering of the bridges. The architectural design of the bridges, on the other hand, was the work of George Dunkelberger, a trained architect whose contribution to the project is perhaps the most conspicuous visual feature of the parkway. To these men and the numerous others who worked under them goes the credit for the Merritt design that ultimately emerged. No one member of the design team can be given the credit – or would have wished to get it – since there was a true spirit of teamwork not only among the design staff but among the construction workers as well. As Earl Wood observed, "I never knew a man who worked on that parkway that did not have a sense of what we were trying to do. They felt they were really making a contribution to Fairfield County and the nation."[4] And on another occasion, Wood stated even more passionately, "The older I grow, the less significant appears to be the desire to get 'credit' for an accomplishment.... It was a tremendous, cooperative venture fired with the enthusiasm of youth. I am sure none of us paid heed then to getting credit for the conception and execution of the project as it unfolded before us."[5] Like many other projects undertaken in the depths of the Depression, this one appears to have engendered a strong sense of comradery and optimism among those devoted to its realization.

If it is virtually impossible to determine the whos and hows of decisions affecting the outcome of the parkway design, the results of that decision making were spelled out by Creamer in his address to the Connecticut Society of Civil Engineers. After describing the route to his colleagues — the eastern terminus was still at the Post Road and the Washington Street bridge in Milford at the time of his presentation — Creamer detailed various design features in considerable technical detail, showing slides of typical cross-sectional drawings. He indicated that the grass shoulders in a cut would be five feet two inches wide, with the tops of the cuts rounded to merge with the original ground plane. Shoulders in fills would be nine feet wide, their "toes" rounded, again to blend in with the original topography. Rustic guardrails, where needed, would be four feet six inches back from the right curb line. The total width of the parkway and its margins in a cut, therefore, would be eighty-four feet eight inches; on a fill, ninety-two feet four inches.

Similarly, Creamer spelled out the narrowing of the median at the pinched bridges. The landscaped strip began to taper from the normal width down to a sixteen-inch concrete curb at 450 feet from the near face of a bridge, reaching the sixteen-inch width at 106 feet from the bridge; the effective width of the pavement over or under the bridge is sixty feet. He was equally thorough in describing the complex system of catch basins, culverts, and storm sewers that insures proper drainage of surface water from the pavements — the storm sewers run under the median strip — and methods for establishing the degree of curvature and the banking of curves. But he neglected to show how the formulas were arrived at and why. The banking of curves, for example, was calculated for speeds then considered safe, only up to forty-five miles an hour. Whether this had to do, however, with the handling characteristics of the cars of the day or the demands of the FCPA that the parkway not be a speedway is unclear. The reasons behind these and other technical design decisions remain a matter of speculation. Fortunately, decisions affecting the parkway's aesthetics are more accessible.

**Dunkelberger's Bridges**          For many, the parkway's sixty-eight original bridges are
the heart of its special appeal. The popular belief is that each is by a different designer. But in fact they are all the work of a single architectural designer, George L.
Dunkelberger. Born in Camden, New Jersey, in 1891, he trained at the Drexel Institute
of Technology in Philadelphia. His naval service in World War I, however, apparently
contributed as much to his technical knowledge as his formal education, and after the
war he began his career as an architect in partnership with Joseph Gelman in Hartford,
Connecticut. After about 1921, he designed mainly apartment and residential work in
the eclectic manner of the interwar period.[6]

With the collapse of the construction industry during the Depression, Dunkelberger
tried first to practice privately out of his home, but finding even that unproductive, he
was forced by 1933 to take what employment he could with the Connecticut Highway
Department as a draftsman in the cartography division. In 1935, he was made a senior
draftsman in the bridge design division, and from there he was transferred to the so-
called Unit 50 – the special task force MacDonald established to work exclusively on
the Merritt project. In his new position he soon impressed his civil engineering superi-
ors and colleagues not only with his drafting skills but with his ability as a designer
as well. He was soon given responsibility for the design of all parkway bridges, under-
taking this assignment with the same good humor and touch of fantasy that had already
established him as a likable, slightly offbeat character around the Highway Department
offices. Dunkelberger was a latter-day Renaissance man who was as skilled as a musi-
cian or cartoonist as he was at solving architectural design problems.

Dunkelberger's design work was essentially cosmetic, since the structural or engineering design of the bridges was the work of Leslie Sumner and his associates and
consisted mostly of simple segmental steel arched bridges with concrete abutments.
Since the pinched width of the parkway pavement was only about sixty feet, the span of
the bridges was not particularly great even by the standards of the time, and the width
of the underpasses, in most cases spanning a two-lane town street, was even narrower.
The bridges, therefore, did not present any major technical challenges, and it is fair to
say that Sumner's work marks no significant engineering breakthrough.

What is new, then, is Dunkelberger's effort to dress up the bridges, to disguise the
monotony of their engineering sameness by making each bridge unique. He did this by
an imaginative treatment of the concrete abutments of each bridge and by the often re-

markable precast panels and poured-in-place concrete work with which he clothed the underlying steel arched girders which are left exposed on only three of the overpasses. By contrast, Westchester's Hutchinson River Parkway has bridges of a single basic design throughout its length. Although the span of a given bridge might vary depending on whether it were an overpass or underpass or one of the many bridges crossing the narrow Hutchinson River, they were all sheathed in quarry-faced native granite whose rugged texture contributed to the picturesque effect of that parkway.

The Hutchinson Parkway had two advantages denied the Merritt. First, it was built under the patronage of Robert Moses, who was hardly the pinchpenny MacDonald was and knew the value of sharing the wealth with others, in this case the Masons and Bricklayers Union. Second, the Hutch was largely completed before the Depression, whereas the Merritt was a product of it – most of the construction workers were paid with WPA funds. Cost cutting was a key to the successful construction of the Merritt from the

*Hutchinson River Parkway, King Street overpass at the Connecticut state line, c. 1940 (Department of Transportation, State of Connecticut).*

outset, and MacDonald and others in Hartford repeatedly rebuffed local demands that more funds be set aside for landscaping the finished road. In answer to a *Bridgeport Post* questionnaire in July 1935, he disclosed that just $250,000 would be allowed for landscaping the thirty-seven miles of highway. When the question was rephrased as "How much should be allowed . . . to retain the natural appearance of the county . . . ?" he responded three million dollars.[7]

In the same questionnaire, MacDonald pegged the average cost of bridge construction at a mere seventy-three thousand dollars each. The follow-up question concerned the added cost to stone-face the bridges, and his answer was unequivocal: nine thousand dollars, or about an eighth of the cost per bridge. Sumner, the project's bridge engineer, was quite specific in isolating added cost as the major factor in the decision to use raw concrete rather than to veneer the bridges: "This sum [about $680,000] was considered sufficiently important to warrant further study as to the possibilities of producing satisfactory designs by the use of other materials. Also there was a possibly egotistical feeling that masonry did not offer the only possible solution and that equally pleasing results could be obtained by the use of other media."[8]

Under the circumstances, it is not surprising that stone was used very sparingly: only three bridges were given that treatment. That stone veneer was considered a frill had already been widely rumored (thus the *Post*'s pointed questions), and property owners along the route were irate that *their* bridges would not be finished in the picturesque manner of the Westchester examples. Helen Binney Kitchel spoke for many in her series of articles on the history of the Merritt Parkway in the *Greenwich Press* in 1938: "When specifications calling for concrete structures were published, disapproval was quickly voiced. The Garden Clubs, Greenwich Woman's Republican Club, Town Plan Commission and other groups [insisted] on stone facing. . . . But in spite of petitions and meetings, our requests and entreaties were parried with the announcement that the cost was prohibitive and that stone bridges could not be built except by contribution of the towns. . . . It seemed to indicate a lack of regard for the appearance of the highway and a lowering of the standards promised."[9] Their demands were ignored by MacDonald, however – except in one case.

The sculptor and painter Gutzon Borglum had his home and studio along the Rippowam River in the Turn of River district of Stamford. Borglum's reputation at the time rested not so much on the unfinished Mount Rushmore project as on the earlier Stone

Mountain carving he had started in Georgia. When money ran out and the patrons tried to scale back on Borglum's proposal for converting the stone escarpment into a monument to the Confederacy, he promptly withdrew his services and sued for breach of contract. These actions bolstered Borglum's reputation as a scrappy, irascible individual who happened to be touched with a certain genius. When Borglum discovered that a concrete bridge was to span the Rippowam within sight of his property, he thundered that if the bridge were not faced in stone, there would be "trouble." [10] It was. Few people have ever seen the result, however, since the parkway overpasses the splendid masonry work Dunkelberger designed, which is hidden in the lush forest glen below. Ironically, Borglum barely had time to enjoy the fruits of his bluster: he died in 1941, only a few years after the bridge was completed.

*Rippowam River bridge, c. 1938 (Department of Transportation, State of Connecticut).*

*Wire Mill Road, Stamford,*
*detail of the Connecticut*
*state seal.*

*Newfield Avenue, Stamford,*
*detail of the Connecticut*
*state seal.*

*Clinton Avenue, Westport,*
*detail of the Connecticut*
*state seal.*

Borglum's bridge aside, the decision to use a pebble-surfaced, raw concrete finish for the bridges held firm. Only the major U.S. Route 7 underpass in Norwalk and the Guinea Road overpass in Stamford were similarly veneered. For the rest, Dunkelberger invented a variety of forms and textures, relying on the plasticity of concrete to produce a collection of bridges that run the gamut from the dramatic to the whimsical. That so many of the bridges are memorable is a credit to his design sense and willingness to experiment. Dunkelberger was not, however, a particularly innovative designer; he had no claim to a national reputation either for his work on the Merritt bridges or in his private practice. Rather, he was able to assimilate ideas from acknowledged leaders in the design field, adapting the concepts they had developed in more conventional architectural contexts to bridge designs. What the bridges may lack in original design concepts, however, is easily offset by the architect's imaginative manipulation of forms, his ability to work with a stipulated material not familiar to him, and an admirable brio that is never predictable.

Many of these bridges reflect his penchant for the Art Deco style, but Dunkelberger was certainly no purist in selecting either the general style or the specific design motifs for his work. On the other hand, Art Deco itself was hardly a model of stylistic purism. David Gebhard, one of Art Deco's leading historians, has identified a number of subspecies of the style, such as Zig-Zag, Streamlined, and WPA Moderne.[11] To these one might add Frank Lloyd Wright's more judgmental term "Disinfected Classic" and the rather florid, curvilinear patterns of the original French version prominently shown in 1925 at the Exposition Internationale des Arts Décoratifs – thus "Art Deco." Above all, it is clear that the sense of order and geometric harmony in most Art Deco owes a large debt to the classicism of the Ecole des Beaux-Arts, from which many of its major figures had graduated. Elements of all of these Art Deco variations appear in the Merritt bridges, as well as some surprisingly pure examples of Beaux-Arts classicism – surprising because Dunkelberger had no apparent training in this tradition and showed in his own pre-Merritt work an affinity for a kind of playful gothic. Along with this eclectic mix, he also contributed some witty inventions of his own, and when he ran out of ideas, he could always fall back on the state seal as a decorative motif.

What can be said about the bridges as a group? The designs were largely dictated by engineering factors – span, alignment of intersecting roads (diagonal or at right angles – none of the bridges are curved), degree of grade on a hill, and so on. Consistent with

Dunkelberger's eclectic design ideas and the free hand he was allowed in the designs, there is no theme, program, or iconography common to the entire project. Some motifs, it is true, were repeated (such as the state seal), and some bridges appear to be close variants of one another. In general, however, each design was an individual concept reflecting the architect's response to the particular site or his whims of the moment. Generally the overpasses are more exuberant and impressive than the underpasses, affording pleasure to parkway users not wasted on cross traffic. This rule has a number of notable exceptions, although the thirty-one underpasses can be seen only by driving the surface roads or walking the river banks below bridges. And unlike modern freeways and much of the modern architecture built along them, where the gestalt of the design can be taken in at freeway speeds, there is a wealth of fine detail on many of the bridges that is lost at even legal speeds, much less the speed that many commuters squeeze out of the parkway's sinuous curves.

The original intention of the FCPA and others was that speeds on the parkway be held down to between thirty and forty-five miles an hour, but the richness of detail is difficult to grasp even at those leisurely speeds. It takes a keen eye to catch what is going on in the open work of the metal balustrade of the Merwins Lane overpass in the town of Fairfield: small butterflies are caught in stylized metal spider webs whose builders are about to devour their hapless captives. The abutments of the same bridge are enriched with much larger concrete butterflies perched on the horizontal striations, although these are often obscured by the verdant underbrush that encroaches on the bridges in the summer, all but obliterating some of Dunkelberger's best efforts. The low relief sculpture on the Comstock Hill Road overpass in Norwalk, the work of the Milford sculptor Edward Ferrari, who contributed embellishments to a number of bridges, is another case in point. Each abutment face is adorned with the bust of a Pilgrim or an Indian, apparent references to New England's colonial past and done in a simplified curvilinear style that recalls the work of Paul Manship, Lee Laurie, and similar Art Deco sculptors. Difficult to read at any time, these reliefs almost disappear into the Connecticut jungle in the summer.

Not all the bridges are so subtle, however. Some use bold forms as the basis of their design, eliminating intricate decorative embellishments. The Morehouse Highway bridge, again in Fairfield, crosses the parkway in a series of steplike sections that march downward from one side of the cut to the other. These steps, in turn, appear

*Merwins Lane overpass,*
*Fairfield.*

to be subdivided into smaller cubical elements as if the entire design were fashioned from a giant-sized set of child's building blocks. This bold motif is most likely derived from the so-called textile block houses designed in Los Angeles in the early 1920s by Frank Lloyd Wright. The Morehouse bridge, of course, is not actually made up of individual blocks as Wright's houses were; rather, the appearance of blocks is an example of Dunkelberger's exploitation of the plastic effects to which poured concrete lends itself. The blocklike units result from a reticulated pattern of thin wooden strips attached to the inner face of the concrete formwork.

Two other bridges, also bold in form, combine strong design with exuberant decoration. They serve as a sort of entrance gate to the east and west ends of the parkway, although neither is precisely at the terminals. The Lake Avenue bridge in Greenwich is unusual in that the metal arches are not shrouded in concrete – one of only three overpasses so treated on the whole parkway. It spans the roadway in two graceful segmental arcs, welcoming travelers to Connecticut and the Merritt with a triumphal arch forever bedecked with cast-iron vines like some twentieth-century Piranesian ruin. The decorative metalwork on this bridge, as on the others that use metal trim, was produced by Kenneth Lynch, a metal craftsman and founder whose contemporary works included the Art Deco stainless steel gargoyles and other fittings on the Chrysler Building. Lynch's studio, then on Long Island, was later relocated a few miles above the parkway on Route 7.[12]

The eastern gateway near the Housatonic River is a willful bit of whimsy, the James Farm Road overpass. In the main, the bridge employs classical elements from the Renaissance vocabulary such as the strongly articulated voussoirs that in fact are again only lines impressed into the concrete, as in the Morehouse bridge. Such details recall the strong debt Art Deco owed to Beaux-Arts classicism. They hardly prepare the traveler, however, for the principal feature of this bridge, a theatrical flourish consisting of two sets of furled Nike wings incongruously parked atop the central pier of the double-arched bridge. Once again the work of sculptor Edward Ferrari, these large forms were cast from his original plaster models and stand on what would otherwise be a rather routine, classicizing design. It is such implausible touches as this – the brash intrusion of the patently man-made into the verdant (but also man-made!) environment –

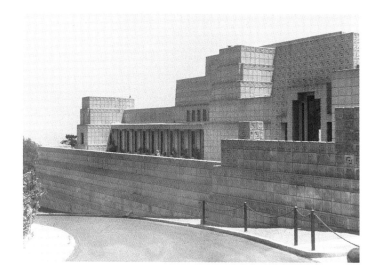

*Morehouse Highway*
*overpass, Fairfield.*

*Frank Lloyd Wright, Ennis*
*House, Los Angeles, 1924.*

*Morehouse Highway,*
*abutment detail.*

that makes driving the Merritt so memorable as opposed to the no-nonsense, functional sameness of the interstate highways.

These examples suggest the range of Dunkelberger's sources and inventions, though it by no means exhausts the variety of his work and his ability to mix and match styles and motifs. His familiarity with Beaux-Arts traditions is unexpected in light of the preference for gothic design elements in his pre-Merritt practice. His use of Beaux-Arts classicism, reflected in varying degrees in perhaps two dozen of the bridges, may offer a clue to his highly eclectic design approach. Whereas his architectural training appears to have emphasized technical rather than aesthetic considerations, he seems to have supplemented his education with a self-taught course in architectural history, much of it derived from books or built examples he could have studied locally. This certainly would have included the work of the country's leading Renaissance Revival architecture firm, McKim, Mead and White, whose prolific work had been the subject of an important monograph published in both trade and student editions in 1915. Since their spectacular successes with the Boston Public Library (1887) and their important contributions to the Chicago Columbian Exposition (1893), McKim, Mead and White had led the renewal of Renaissance ideals that informed banks, schools, government, and a host of other building types over the next four decades. Some of Dunkelberger's bridges do echo McKim, Mead and White's Memorial (Arlington) Bridge across the Potomac in Washington, D.C., an opus he could hardly not have known since its completion in 1932 garnered extensive coverage in the professional press.[13]

Like many architects of a lesser talent, Dunkelberger apparently relied on published works of others for inspiration. Just as Wright was the muse for the Morehouse design, so Greenwich's stone-faced Guinea (formerly Rocky Craig) Road overpass shows a marked affinity for the late nineteenth-century work of Henry Hobson Richardson. The rough granite boulders Richardson used in the Ames Gate house (1880) or in the Paine house (1884), as well as his penchant for powerful, cyclopian masonry seen in the Allegheny County Courthouse (1883), are reviewed in the massive voussoirs and slightly less forceful infill of random rubble masonry in the spandrels and balustrades on the Guinea bridge. The difference between Richardson and Dunkelberger, however, is that Richardson used masonry as structure and the color and texture of the stone as integral ornament; Dunkelberger's masonry is pure decoration, a coat of stone hung on the underlying steel armature.

James Farm Road overpass,
Stratford.

James Farm Road overpass,
detail of Nike wings. (Department of Transportation, State
of Connecticut).

*Guinea (formerly Rocky Craig) Road overpass, Greenwich, c. 1940 (Department of Transportation, State of Connecticut).*

*North Street overpass, Greenwich, c. 1940 (Department of Transportation, State of Connecticut).*

Given this remarkable range of styles – from classical revival and romantic Richard-sonian romanesque to Wright's high-tech constructivism and assorted Art Deco em-bellishments – the question inevitably arises as to how a design for any specific bridge was worked out. In the first place, Dunkelberger stated in an address to the Connecticut Society of Civil Engineers in 1942 that his work was subordinate to that of the engi-neers, and that he took his cues from their technical demands as to general form. He was no less clear, however, that the "one principle which should be considered . . . is the incorporation of the existing landscape in the problem."[14] To this end, he would hike the stake line of a newly surveyed section of road to study the general topography. When the site of a bridge was excavated, he would return and make several sketches, often variants of the same basic design concept. He would then develop these into a series of perspective renderings and elevations that were shown to the engineers and other staffers and from which a selection was made. Earl Wood indicated that in most cases it was Dunkelberger himself who made the final decision, although in some cases suggestions for additions or changes or even for combinations of elements from several alternatives might be made. Once the final version was approved, however, he refused to entertain the slightest deviation or compromise in the design.[15]

There is a theater-like aspect to many of his bridges. That is, instead of simply de-signing a bridge to span the parkway between opposing abutments, Dunkelberger con-ceived bridge, abutments, and attendant landscaping as a unit, a stage set to enhance the "drama" of driving through, as he put it, "some of the finest country we have in Connecticut."[16] This stage scenery, then, was intended not to compete with the natural setting but to enhance or even express it. This reflects the architect's notion that the bridges should be integrated into the natural landscape, a concept close to Wright's phi-losophy of organic architecture. It suggests that the similarity of the Morehouse High-way bridge to Wright's block houses is no accident. Dunkelberger, incidentally, titled his talk to the Connecticut civil engineers quite simply "Highway Architecture," and throughout the talk he used this locution to refer to his bridges. Clearly Dunkelberger conceived the spans as pieces of architecture, not just utilitarian structures, and that in addition to "commodity" and "firmness," in the charming phrase of Sir Henry Wotton, they also possess "delight." And if this could best be provided by resort to theatrical devices, Dunkelberger had no objection, a philosophical stand he shared with many major architects, Wright not excepted.

The analogy to the theater is not only evident in the "staging" of some of the most

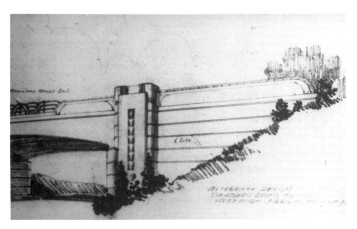

*Danbury Road underpass, Westport, proposed design, c. 1936 (Department of Transportation, State of Connecticut).*

*Danbury Road underpass, alternate design, c. 1936 (Department of Transportation, State of Connecticut).*

*Merwins Lane overpass, Fairfield, proposed design, c. 1936 (Department of Transportation, State of Connecticut).*

*Merwins Lane overpass, alternate design, c. 1936 (Department of Transportation, State of Connecticut).*

successful bridges – the way they suddenly appear around a corner or over a hill – but also in the way they often reach out to embrace the landscape from which they spring. The Wire Mill Road overpass in Stamford is a good example. Although the main design elements are essentially classical – the squared balusters, the dentil course running the length of the span, the centrally placed cartouche (the state seal) around which the design is symmetrical – the abutments are anything but classical. They curve out sinuously to meet the landscape much as the apron of a stage curves outward into the auditorium to bring actor and audience into closer contact.[17]

If the dramatic staging of the bridges was an important design element, Dunkelberger also made very clear what he meant by integrating the design with the landscape, his version of "organic architecture." "In low, flat country," he said, "the design should typify the character of the landscape, perhaps by horizontal lines; in rolling country, by the addition of a few verticals; and on rough terrain, a combination of the two with neither predominating, I am sure, would result in a pleasing structure. Of course, we find rough country at times where the use of verticals only would be satisfactory." That this was intended to create "delight" is also clear: whereas some "engineers and architects... believe that all structures should be functional in their design... I prefer to consider the individuality of structure from the standpoint of what I think would be most pleasing to the general public in an architectural sense."[18]

That the Merritt bridges are uneven in their pursuit of delight is evident. At times some approach the effects of an English folly, the garden ornament that is an end in itself, as in the Nike wings of the James Farm overpass. Other structures such as the Easton Road (Route 136) underpass in Westport seem more melodramatic than dramatic in the heavy-handed, Piranesian scale of the elements. A certain mannerism is evident in the treatment of the Huntington Road underpass in Stratford. And some are merely bland – the Cutspring Road underpass, also in Stratford. Comparing the delicate iron vine motive of the Lake Avenue bridge in Greenwich with the badly scaled and somewhat comical vegetation that "grows" around the steel supports of the Route 110 underpass in Stratford shows what wild swings of creative output Dunkelberger was capable of. To his credit, he recognized that not all of his designs were equally compelling: "We have a few ornaments on the tops of the piers [of the Grassy Hill Road bridge], and, after they were placed, I felt they weren't so hot, and I still feel so. But you can't do something that is halfway decent without inserting something that is not so good in between once in a while. . . . I want to take all the blame myself."[19]

Easton Road underpass,
Westport.

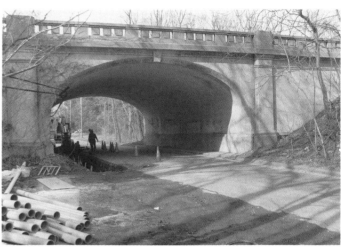

Perry Avenue underpass,
Norwalk.

Huntington Road underpass,
Stratford.

*River Road (Route 110)*
*underpass, Stratford, detail*
*of "foliage."*

In his best designs, however, Dunkelberger created truly memorable "highway architecture." And although there are those who prefer the calm and repose of the classically inspired bridges, most parkway users, asked to nominate their favorite, would probably select one of the Art Deco designs. These lively works show more clearly how Dunkelberger exploited the plastic possibilities of his medium than do those where he was simply translating historical masonry motifs into concrete.

Most of the Art Deco effects were achieved by one of two means. Dunkelberger most frequently used poured-in-place concrete, where the usually smooth formwork was modified with plaster molds, wood strips, or lapped boards similar to inverted clapboard siding to create integral patterns in the concrete. Where a more dramatic, architectonic effect was desired, the forms themselves might be shaped into elaborate three-dimensional structures. Alternatively, decoration or sculpture in metal or concrete was applied rather like wallpaper. If metal, the decoration was made of cast iron and bolted in place. If concrete, the work was usually done in thin, two-inch precast reinforced slabs, some as large as five by nine feet, which were then hung from the steel frame of the bridge or the poured concrete abutments like the curtain wall of a skyscraper; these were then secured with tie screws and lock nuts at the back of the panel. To insure quality control, the panels were prefabricated in a shop on Long Island, not cast in the field. Because they were vibrated into a dense concrete, they have generally stood up to the effects of weathering, particularly winter freezing, better than the more porous poured-in-place concrete.

Two excellent examples of cast-in-place work where a particularly strong horizontal effect was achieved using the clapboard technique are the overpasses at Main Street in Trumbull and Merwins Lane in Fairfield. Both are located on fairly flat terrain. The vertical emphasis Dunkelberger advocated for more rolling sites is found on the abutments of numerous bridges. It is less common, however, on the spans themselves, where the relatively shallow depth of the arch did not lend itself to vertical treatment. The overpasses at Burr Street in Fairfield and Lapham Road in New Canaan, for example, use closely spaced vertical striations that recall the fluting of a classical pilaster without being imitative.

A number of abutments handled with extreme plasticity stand out. In such cases, the complex forms were constructed to give the abutments the profile of that most important and typical of Art Deco designs, the 1920s setback skyscraper. The overpasses

Main Street overpass,
Trumbull.

North Avenue overpass,
Westport, c. 1940. (Department of Transportation, State
of Connecticut).

*Lapham Road overpass, New Canaan, c. 1940 (Department of Transportation, State of Connecticut).*

*Congress Street overpass, Fairfield (Department of Transportation, State of Connecticut).* **top left**

*MetroNorth New Canaan Line overpass, c. 1940 (Department of Transportation, State of Connecticut).*

*Stamford Avenue underpass, New Canaan.* **bottom right**

at Riverbank Road in Stamford and Congress Street in Fairfield evoke the power and drama that Hugh Ferris, the preeminent architectural renderer of the period, brought to drawings of highrise buildings in the 1920s – a power and drama more evident in his drawings than in the executed buildings themselves. Another example, striking in the simplicity of its abutment design, is the overpass of the New Canaan Line of the old New York–New Haven Railroad. The skyscraper motive was also used for a number of underpasses, such as at Silvermine Avenue in Norwalk and Black Rock Turnpike (Route 58) in Fairfield.

Applied decoration on the abutments runs the gamut from the Indians and Pilgrims on the Comstock Hill bridge in Norwalk, done in the lightweight precast panel technique, to the cast-iron grill motif that adorned the late Huntington Turnpike overpass in Trumbull (demolished to make way for the routes 8 and 25 interchange). Precast figural sculpture appears on several other bridges as well, such as Fairfield's Burr Street overpass, Ferrari's tribute to the engineers and construction workers of the Merritt. Plant forms were another favorite Dunkelberger motif, whether the fairly literal translations of the cast-iron vines on the Lake Avenue overpass or the much more abstract giant concrete hollyhocks – perhaps reflecting Wright's use of the same flower in the 1917 Barnsdall house in Los Angeles – that grow up the abutments of the Darien–New Canaan Road (Route 124) bridge. This design is typical of the "gilded lily" subgenre that the architect sometimes adopted: the decorative hollyhocks are applied to another of the setback skyscraper abutments and reflect them in their configuration. Each successful in its own right, the two combined have a curious redundancy.

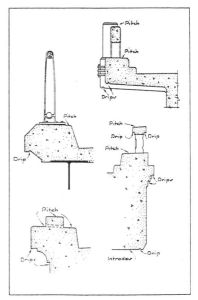

*Technical drawing of drip moulding to prevent rain runoff from washing across concrete surfaces.*

Dunkelberger experimented with a number of other means, both technical and formal, of varying the bridges. Among the purely technical aspects were a variety of ways of coping with the problem of water runoff. Poured concrete is vulnerable to staining when rainwater washes across its surface, and to prevent this, pitched surfaces and drip moldings were integrally cast with the balusters, spandrels, and soffits. Although virtually unseen by passersby, the effects are apparent in the absence of staining. He and the engineers and contractors also tried different combinations of aggregates to achieve the rich yet subtle surface effects seen in the bridges. Quartz was used to add a touch of glint, but the overall buff tonality that makes the bridges blend into the landscape resulted from aggregates selected for their earth tones. The bridges' slightly rough, pebbly texture came from exposing the aggregate rather than allowing the usual smooth sur-

Comstock Hill overpass,
Norwalk.

Comstock Hill, detail of
Pilgrim relief.

Former Huntington Turn-
pike overpass, Trumbull,
detail of cast-iron ornament
now attached to Route 108
overpass.

face typical of poured concrete to develop. Similarly, the original colors of paint used on exposed structural ribs, railings, and other nonconcrete elements (now mainly lost in later repainting) consisted not of what Dunkelberger called "gloomy blacks and uninteresting grays" but of a harmonious combination of warm greens, grays, browns, and reds – a palette of earth tones intended to enliven the bridges while blending them into the landscape. The starling blue that the Lake Avenue bridge is now painted is not what he had in mind.

Other interesting techniques tried on several bridges included scrafito work where the surface concrete was removed to reveal an underlying layer of contrasting aggregate. Both the North Avenue bridge in Westport and the Grumman Avenue bridge in Norwalk incorporate Wisconsin black onyx and Swedish emerald pearl aggregates to create bold patterns – distinctly Art Deco in the case of North Avenue, whose verticality is echoed in the striations of both abutments and balustrades. A few bridges used a color-infusing technique called the Cleveland Lithichrome process: dry mineral color was blown into the open pores of patterns sandblasted into the surface and sealed with liquid silica. The white classical vase motif set on a Wedgwood blue field seen on the Marvin Ridge Road overpass in New Canaan is an example of this technique. And in response to the never stilled demand for stone-faced bridges, Dunkelberger and his colleagues experimented with cast-concrete facings – the thin-panel technique – that "creates the atmosphere of the stone bridge with the economy of . . . concrete," as he put it.[20] Many observers, including scholars, have been tricked by the trompe l'oeil illusion, which appears on the Newtown Avenue overpass in Westport and the Frenchtown Road bridge in Trumbull. The former uses strong Art Deco elements, the latter a double-arched crossing that relies principally on its random ashlar "stone" facing for visual effect.

Dunkelberger also employed some formal inventions that recall traditional architectural elements but without the original intent or context. These inventions often have an Art Deco flavor. One recurrent theme used as a balustrade detail is derived from the merlons and crenelles of medieval fortifications, perhaps a throwback to the architect's penchant for the gothic. North Avenue in Westport, Lapham Road in New Canaan, and Burr Street in Fairfield all show this motif, and variations appear at Reading Road in Fairfield, where the slits between crenelles are omitted, and Comstock Hill Road in Norwalk and Route 124 in New Canaan, where a crenelled pattern emerges from the saw-toothed treatment of the balustrade. More distant but still related are the hand-

*North Avenue overpass, Westport, detail of balustrade.*

*Detail of aggregate surface, Milford Connector, bridge over the Post Road, Milford.*

North Avenue, abutment
detail. **top left**

Marvin Ridge Road overpass,
New Canaan, c. 1940. (De-
partment of Transportation,
State of Connecticut). **top
right**

Newtown Avenue overpass,
Westport, c. 1940. (Department of Transportation, State
of Connecticut). **center**

Frenchtown Road overpass,
Trumbull, c. 1940 (Department of Transportation, State
of Connecticut). **bottom**

some, undulating forms of the Madison Avenue overpass in Trumbull, a design made more charming by whimsical, scroll-like vegetal forms in which both the wings and bastions of the abutments terminate, curvilinear touches that look as if a master patissier had completed the decoration of a cake with a deft swirl.

In the more utilitarian structures Dunkelberger's talents seem less evident. Underpasses little seen even by those driving on the surface streets, such as the spans over rivers or railroad tunnels, often are curiously plain. The steel arched span over the Saugatuck River in Westport, at 135 feet the longest bridge on the parkway, might have been a real opportunity for Dunkelberger because of its scale; but curiously it lacks his usual touch, and Metro North's Danbury line underpasses the parkway near Route 7 with little ceremony and less charm. The Housatonic River bridge, longer than the Saugatuck bridge but not technically part of the Merritt, is a competent piece of engineering but also seems to lack those special qualities that would make it "highway architecture." Many drivers would even question its engineering wisdom: the open-grid steel deck, a slick surface that can make a car fishtail, has caught many motorists off guard. Dunkelberger did indeed work on the Housatonic bridge, an afterthought made in 1938 when the parkway was extended northward to Hartford as the Wilbur Cross Parkway, but there is little visual evidence of his hand.

*Saugatuck River bridge, Westport.* **left**

*New Canaan–Darien Road overpass, New Canaan, balustrade detail.*

*Housatonic River bridge,
Stratford-Milford.*

*Norwalk River bridge,
Norwalk.* **right**

Another bridge that apparently escaped Dunkelberger's touch but remains a strong and compelling form is the triple-arched Norwalk River bridge between the Danbury Line and Route 7. Simple engineering at its best, these three half-circular barrel vaults of smooth concrete have a direct relationship of form and function that appeals to contemporary taste but exhibits little of Dunkelberger's usual "delight." His real legacy, of course, consists of the more visible bridges, the overpasses that regularly cross the parkway.

**Earl Wood & the Parkway Landscaping**     If Dunkelberger's bridges are among the most memorable aspects of the parkway, the landscaping, by contrast, seems to play a decidedly secondary role. Like a supernumerary in a stage production, its presence is essential, but it plays a nonspeaking part. Earl Wood, the engineer in charge of landscaping and roadside development, would take this as high praise of his work since landscaping was, for him, most successful when it was least noticed, when it blended subtly with the natural environment. Writing in 1937 in *Connecticut Woodlands*, the journal of the Connecticut Forest and Park Association, he stated his goal succinctly: "The main objective of the landscaping program has been to assist nature in healing the scars of construction."[21] His success may be measured by the degree to which the landscaping goes unnoticed.

Wood and his staff began planning the landscaping before the start of road construction, and their efforts continued side by side with the actual rough grading of the route, culminating in the sodding and replanting of the finished parkway. From the beginning, Wood was determined to make the completed road look as if it had always been there, a momentary interruption in the flow of the natural setting not so much attracting attention to itself as providing a new way of seeing the natural beauty of southern Connecticut.

Wood had studied forestry at Syracuse University before joining the Connecticut Highway Department. When fears that the new road would end up as just another ugly highway led to calls for careful landscape planning, Wood was tapped for the assignment. He was not a trained landscape architect, however. Much of the credit for translating his ideas into a green reality must go to Weld Thayer Chase, who *was* a trained landscape architect. Chase, who grew up in Newport, Rhode Island, was first intro-

*View from Lapham Street overpass looking west, New Canaan, c. 1940 (Department of Transportation, State of Connecticut).*

duced to gardening when as a teenager he worked on the grounds of the grand Newport estates.[22] Later he studied botany at Rhode Island State College and, after graduation, landscape architecture, then a new field, at the University of Massachusetts. He finished his schooling in the midst of the Depression, so, with no prospects of a job, he spent some five months cycling in England and on the Continent to study the great parks and gardens of Europe. In 1935, at age twenty-six, he was hired as the Highway Department's first trained landscape architect and was immediately assigned to Earl Wood's team.

While Wood had a good idea of what he wanted, his lack of specific training made achieving his vision difficult. In Chase he recognized a young man with the expertise he himself lacked, and he turned over to Chase the design of the entire Merritt landscaping scheme. Thus, the two most obvious visual elements of the parkway – its bridges and its landscaping – ultimately proved to be the work of only two men – assisted, to be sure, by a host of able engineers and other technicians.

Chase clearly understood Wood's desire to rely on native species rather than exotic plant materials, and his academic background in botany made him an especially apt appointee. Not only was he responsible for the broad plan for the entire project, but he also selected the exact location for each major new tree, pounding labeled stakes in the ground to instruct the planting crew. He also cajoled the engineers into saving extant trees along the route and into trimming cuts a bit here or making fills a little more rounded and gentle there, all in the name of aesthetic effect, not engineering efficiency. His design method was simple and intuitive: he worked on sets of large engineering drawings provided by Warren Creamer's department, introducing his own "landscaping plans over the base drawings."[23] In the placement of trees he responded to topographical and man-made features of the site, but there seems to have been no formula: he used a given species here or there based on what looked right to his mind's eye. On at least one occasion, he also executed a model of a section of the finished landscaping, although this appears to have been more a demonstration of what his work would look like than a design technique.[24]

When a new section of construction began, Wood, Chase, and their men would scout the route, marking fine native specimens to be saved from the bulldozers. Trained foresters from the Highway Department then supervised the tree-cutting operation in advance of excavation work to insure preservation of trees and plants not actually in the way of construction. Their efforts did not stop there, however. To keep the replanting as close as possible to the natural order, the landscape crew dug up small shrubs and saplings from the actual route and relocated them to temporary nurseries along the way; then they were replanted at the site after construction was completed. Similarly, loam from the construction strip was scraped up and stockpiled nearby to be used in reestablishing the natural growth rather than as fill. This environmental concern saved not only the topsoil but, dear to MacDonald's parsimonious heart, the money that otherwise would have been ticketed to replace it.

Such conservation efforts took on a life of their own as Wood and his crew began scouting nearby areas for other native plant materials that might become available. Construction of the Edgewood Country Club in Cromwell meant the imminent destruction of some one thousand mature dogwood trees native to the site. Quick action saved them for later replanting along the parkway.[25] Private donations of plant materials were also accepted. In the end, Wood had amassed some quarter million trees and shrubs that were planted along the finished highway. A special sod farm was also started so that the median, shoulders, and fills could be sodded as soon as construction ended to prevent erosion and reintroduce grasses similar to the native meadow varieties.

Concern for the environment and efforts to enhance the motorists' experience of it took other forms as well. A potential vista at the crest of a hill or on a gentle curve might be brought out by removing or pruning the existing trees along the border, although most of these vistas have since been lost again to Connecticut's verdant forests. The most singular example of such man-made enhancements was the creation of a small lake in Greenwich prosaically known as Toll Gate Pond. (This should not be confused with Putnam Lake, a natural body of water, a few miles further east in Greenwich.) The contractor on this section of the parkway was authorized to excavate gravel for the road from the riverbed of the Byram River. The Byram was later diverted into the cavity and the shores were carefully landscaped. As Wood noted, "With a minimum of expense and effort, a new scenic point of interest was thus created" alongside the parkway.[26]

For Wood and others, the jagged outcroppings that resulted from blasting through the rock ridges along the route were especially ugly scars that needed cosmetic work. Where possible, pockets of earth were developed in the rock cuts and "native rambling vines have been planted on the ledges to soften the harsh appearance."[27] With time, a natural patina has further softened the freshly exposed stone so that today the cuts look almost the same as the natural outcroppings of New England granite that occur along the route. Ironically, the rather crude blasting techniques of the day produced an irregular, almost natural effect very different from the current practice of drilling long, parallel, closely marshaled holes to place the explosive, which produces the sheer, corduroy-like cliffs that hem in many modern highways.

The use of "native rambling vines" – Wood did not list species – offers a clue to the entire landscaping scheme. Not only were plants rescued from destruction by the grading equipment, but Wood and Chase insisted, against the advice and demands of some, that all plantings be native species, not exotics foreign to southern Connecticut.[28] These included pink mountain laurel, the official state flower, as well as dogwoods, gray birch, red cedar, various oaks and maples, and other native hardwoods and conifers. In addition, ferns, wild flowers, and other low shrubs and ground cover plants such as azaleas, black alder, and bayberry were used in an effort to re-create the environment disrupted by construction. These were planted in clusters or as single specimens, but never in

*Rock cut, looking east toward Lapham Road overpass, Greenwich, c. 1938 (Department of Transportation, State of Connecticut).*

rows or other obviously man-made patterns. These plants may seem too small for the context, but they were meant to contribute to a natural ensemble, not stand on their own. An exception to the native-plant rule was the use of Hall's Japanese honeysuckle, a hybrid whose runners put down roots every few feet to make a dense mat that binds the soil on steep fills.

Dealing with Dunkelberger's bridges presented a special challenge since some planting was needed to help them blend in. Hiding them in a jungle, however, was never intended, as the architect's renderings and early photos of the parkway show. Chase solved the problem of revealing the abutments of the bridges by planting low, spreading shrubs as ground cover near the bridges and larger trees in clusters angling back from the abutments. The landscaping thus led the eye to the bridges without masking them. This also meant that for drivers the larger trees acted as a natural warning device, especially at night, by catching headlights and indicating that something lay ahead even before the motorist cleared a hill or curve to see the actual bridge. Similarly, the median strip was planted with great care to continue the informal design approach used along the length of the parkway. At the same time, the vegetation had to be controlled to prevent it from impinging on the sight lines of traffic. For this reason, and because of the complex drainage system, much of the median strip was simply planted in grass with, as Wood put it, "a sprinkling of trees here and there to break up the sameness and repetition of the greensward."[29] These median trees and those planted near the edges of the parkway played a role that went beyond simply breaking the monotony of the central strip or even contributing to a romantic environmental effect: the overarching canopy of branches helped cut glare from the original gleaming white concrete surface.

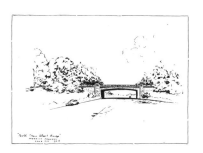

*Thayer Chase drawing for Main Street overpass, Trumbull, c. 1937 (Earl Wood Collection).*

Wood's responsibility also extended to such roadside features as guardrails. These were used principally on the fills and on some of the exit and entrance ramps. The first guardrails, long since replaced by stronger, safer devices, consisted of hand-hewn oak posts and rails, stained a dark brown to preserve the wood and to blend in with the natural setting. On relatively low fills, the guards were only one rail high, about the height of a car's axle; on steeper embankments the guards were two rails high.[30] Apparently these barriers were conceived more as warnings to the motorist of impending danger than as a serious attempt to prevent cars from plunging down the embankments. And there were no guardrails down the center divider at all: the concrete curb, which originally had glass reflectors built into slotted grooves – an innovation for the time but now buried under layers of blacktop – was the sole separation of the opposing traffic lanes.

Finally, Wood's charm and diplomacy soon resulted in his serving as a kind of unofficial ombudsman between the construction project and the communities it passed through. Whether an irate individual worried about the preservation of a favorite tree or a local garden club wanted to "help" with the landscaping, it was Wood who made the rough places smooth. He was able to turn antagonism into cooperation, getting garden clubs to contribute plant material to his nursery without letting them interfere with Chase's grand scheme by introducing foreign plant material or layouts incompatible with his naturalism.[31]

*Looking west toward High Ridge Road, Stamford, c. 1940 (Department of Transportation, State of Connecticut).*

*U.S. Highway 7 interchange, Norwalk, c. 1940 (Department of Transportation, State of Connecticut).*

*View near North Street, Greenwich, c. 1940 (Department of Transportation, State of Connecticut).*

*"Ripples Cut," Greenwich, before landscaping, c. 1935 (Thayer Chase).*

*"Ripples Cut" after land-scaping, c. 1936 (Chase photo).*

*Looking east toward Wire Mill Road, Stamford, c. 1940 (Department of Transportation, State of Connecticut).*

The parkway as it began to take shape around 1936 and 1937, when the first segments were completed, already suggested the remarkable synergy that was to characterize the finished project a few years later. The civil-engineering aspects under the aegis of Warren Creamer and his colleagues provided a model of highway construction unparalleled in its time. George Dunkelberger and Thayer Chase elevated the project from engineering excellence to an integration of all its parts. The aesthetic experience they produced combined architecture, sculpture, and landscaping. The results of their cooperative venture – and especially Chase's marvelously sensitive contribution – can be seen in before-and-after photos of the parkway: the plantings even in their youthful state give focus to the man-made forms. Consciously or not, they created not just a great highway, but also a great work of art.

PICTURE
TOUR
OF THE
MERRITT
PARKWAY

1

2

For landscape engineer Earl Wood, landscaping was most successful when it blended subtly with the natural environment. Here the Park Avenue overpass in Fairfield seems to have "grown" into its winter setting (1) and a demonstrative dogwood, one of the few survivors of the dogwood blight and the effects of auto pollution, announces early spring along the roadside (2).

3

4

5

6

George Dunkelberger's sixty-eight bridges are for many the heart of the parkway's appeal. Pictured are the Lapham Road overpass in New Canaan (3, 4) and the Comstock Hill Road overpass in Norwalk (5, 6). The low relief sculpture on the abutments of the latter are the work of the sculptor Edward Ferrari and represent Indians and pilgrims—references to Connecticut's colonial past.

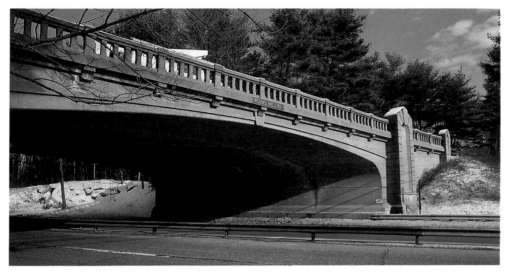

7

8

Dunkelberger conceived the bridges,
abutments, and surrounding landscape
as a unit, an idea he hoped would enhance the drama of driving through
what he called "some of the finest country we have in Connecticut." Round Hill
Road overpass in Greenwich (7), Newfield Avenue overpass in Greenwich (8),
and Guinea Road overpass in Stamford
(9) are shown here, the latter one of
only three stone-veneer bridges on the
parkway.

9

10

11

12

13

14

The similarity of the simple steel-arched bridges is disguised by Dunkelberger's imaginative concrete work on the pylons, balustrades, and abutments. The Riverbank Road overpass in Stamford is shown here, with details of the balustrade and decorated side walls under the bridge (10, 11, 12).

The New Canaan Avenue overpass in New Canaan (13) displays some of the few gothic details in the parkway's architecture, while Art Deco ornament is featured on the Long Ridge Road overpass in Stamford (14).

15

16

The thirty-one underpasses of the parkway, although less dramatic than the overpasses, display special touches as well. Pictured here are the U.S. Route 7 underpass in Norwalk (15)—another of the stone-veneered designs—and the Connecticut Route 136 underpass in Westport (16).

The Lake Avenue overpass in Greenwich (17), near the western end of the parkway, is one of only three bridges whose steel arches are not covered with concrete. The intense blue paint is not original.

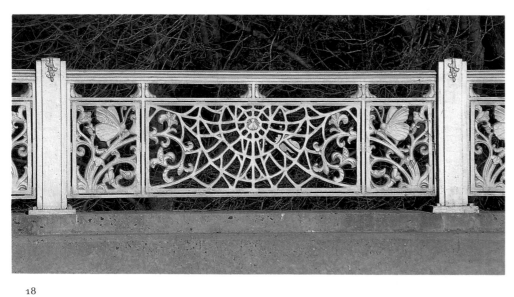

18

19

20

21

The Merwin's Lane overpass (18, 19, 20) combines decorative ironwork and a strong horizontal clapboarding effect. The whimsical theme of the ironwork features small butterflies trapped in a stylized spider's web; larger concrete butterflies are perched on the abutments.

In the Art Deco profiles of the North Avenue overpass in Westport (21, 22) Dunkelberger used the strong vertical emphasis he advocated for bridges in hilly or rugged terrain. The abutments are decorated with sgraffito work.

22

23

24

Some of the underpasses can be viewed only from the riverbanks below the bridges. Pictured here are the Rippowam River bridge (23) and the Saugatuck River bridge, which at 135 feet is the parkway's largest bridge span (25). Nor do many get to see the charms of Toll Gate Pond (24), a man-made feature of the landscape in Greenwich.

25

From rectilinear to whimsical to Art Deco forms: a sculpture niche sans sculpture on the Sport Hill Road overpass in Fairfield (26), an owl about to swoop down on its prey from the Hillside Road overpass in Fairfield (27), and a sunburst pattern of chevrons from the East Rocks Road overpass in Norwalk (28).

29

30

*The curvilinear forms of the hand-
some undulating facade of the Madison
Avenue overpass in Trumbull (29) are
echoed in the road's own gentle curves
(30) and in the bridge abutments that
terminate with a deft swirl (31).*

31

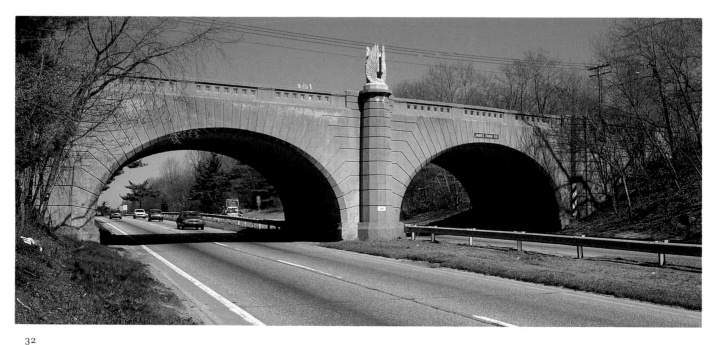

32

33

Two pairs of whimsical six-foot-tall Nike wings (by the sculptor Edward Ferrari) atop the James Farm Road overpass near the eastern end of the parkway in Stratford (32, 33).

Architecture, sculpture, and landscaping combine to make the Merritt Parkway not just a roadway but a work of art. Here, in an autumn setting, is the Burr Street overpass in Fairfield (34, 35) with Ferrari's reliefs commemorating the engineers who built the parkway.

34

35

# 5

## THE PARKWAY'S EARLY HISTORY & LATER DEVELOPMENT

Construction on the parkway took off once the federal pump-priming funds were made available and the county bonds were sold.[1] Depression-strapped private contractors were selected by competitive bidding and awarded approximately seven-mile segments. The work provided jobs for some two thousand workers hired off the dole at a salary of about four thousand dollars a year. With crews working at both ends toward the center, surveying, clearing, or actual construction seemed to be going on everywhere. The professional and popular response when the first seventeen and a half miles were opened to the public in 1938 was quick and mainly enthusiastic. There were also detractors, especially in the engineering fraternity, who raised serious questions about the new road. One doubter, a highly visible protégé of Governor Cross, seems to have been motivated as much by personal ambition and pique as by real misgivings about MacDonald's achievement.

The intent of Cross's administrative reform program was to empower the governor by making agency heads report to him directly instead of operating, often competitively, as autonomous fiefdoms. As part of these reforms a new post was created, director of public works, who was to oversee all state buildings and property, including highways and bridges. Hence MacDonald's Highway Department now came under the purview of the new agency – or so Governor Cross and Robert Hurley, the public works director appointed in July 1937, believed.[2] Rather than submit to this new order, MacDonald marshaled his forces in Hartford in an effort to maintain the independence of his domain. The result was an epic internecine battle. Hurley drew the first blood when he submitted a slashing hundred-page report to Cross attacking MacDonald's stewardship, focusing especially on the Merritt Parkway project. He cited mismanagement, incompetence, and waste of public funds (including the Kemp scandal, which had broken in the press by this time), and laid unnecessarily vicious ad hominem charges.[3]

To demonstrate MacDonald's engineering inadequacies, he said that an old oak tree had been left standing for scenic effect. This required the roadway to be bent around it, thus creating a potential hazard that any responsible engineer would have anticipated. The charge was documented with photographs that showed the tree intruding upon the sharply veering pavement. In fact, the tree had been preserved not only as scenic enhancement but also, perhaps sentimentally, as part of the land acquisition agreement with the Lapham estate in Greenwich. The Laphams had long admired the majestic old oak and urged that it be saved, a request seconded by the New Canaan Garden Club.[4]

*Toll booth, Greenwich, c. 1942 (Department of Transportation, State of Connecticut).* **opposite top**

*Huntington Turnpike overpass, Trumbull, 1990.* **opposite bottom**

The tree proved to be exactly on the projected route, so the planners edged the roadbed out of the intended alignment to preserve the tree and pacify the Lapham family, whose patriarch, the principal promoter of the tree's preservation, had recently died.

MacDonald was stung by the Hurley report's savageness as much as by the charges themselves, and he fought back with a point-by-point rebuttal. In the case of the misplaced oak tree, he sent out his own staff photographers to disprove the allegation by showing that although the tree was near the edge of the parkway, the apparent bending of the roadway was greatly exaggerated in Hurley's documentation. Hurley had, in effect, used trick photography to make his charge more dramatic, according to MacDonald. Meanwhile, Hurley's report was leaked to the press, who had not had such good copy on the parkway since the Kemp land fraud story. The *Bridgeport Post* sent its own photographers to the site of the offending tree and produced a pair of photographs, one "proving" Hurley's contention, the other proving MacDonald's.[5]

In March 1938, three months before the parkway was opened to the public, Governor Cross was forced into the fray. He had his chauffeur drive him past the debated tree twice. Then, Solomon-like, he informed the waiting press and public that both men were correct, but that one "must stand in the right place with the camera" to make them correct. He acknowledged that a jog had been made to save the tree, but said he did not think that this constituted a hazard. "It's a rather nice tree," he added blandly. "But if it is trimmed properly I don't see how it can be a menace."[6] And so he left the issue.

Connecticut superior court judge John A. Cornell, meanwhile, ruled in twisted legalese that highways were not "public works" within the meaning of the recent government reorganization legislation, which spoke of the state's "real assets" as being the public works director's domain. This Democratic legislation had been quickly endorsed by the Republican-controlled state assembly in a complex exchange for judicial appointments. Only later was it realized that this wording effectively delivered control of the Highway Department into the hands of Cross's Democratic appointee to the public works directorship, Hurley. Cornell's decision was apparently bolstered when the governor himself came out in support of it, not wanting to jostle his unstable alliance with the assembly leadership upon which other aspects of his reform program rested. The complex maneuvering was resolved when Cornell's opinion was upheld by the Republican-dominated state Supreme Court of Errors, thus preserving MacDonald's shaky empire.[7]

BRIDGEPORT, CONN. TUESDAY, MARCH 1, 1938    Leads

## 'Trick Photography', Says Macdonald

Highway Commissioner John A. Macdonald, replying to Public Works Commissioner Robert A. Hurley's criticism of his department, says camera tricks were employed to distort Hurley's pictures of Merritt Parkway work. Top picture is from Hurley's report, purporting to show how the roadway line was changed to save a tree in New Canaan. Lower picture is what Macdonald says is a "normal" view of the roadway at that point. Other pictures from both reports will be found on Page 4.

*Lapham Oak intruding and not intruding on roadway (Bridgeport Post).*

His political friends in Hartford could not insulate him from the heat of the Kemp scandal, however. On April 28, 1938, a grand jury charged to investigate the Kemp scandal submitted its findings, among other things calling for the "immediate removal" of MacDonald, and on April 30 Cross asked for his resignation. MacDonald was never implicated in the fraud, but his failure to maintain a tighter reign on Kemp forced him from office in disgrace and lent credence to Hurley's charges. Cross's failure to act sooner was typical of his hesitant decision making, although he obviously had been giving serious thought to the problem: on the day MacDonald resigned, Cross announced the "surprise appointment" of William Junkin Cox, a registered Democrat but politically nonaligned Yale professor of civil engineering, as the new highway commissioner.[8]

Cox's appointment was hailed in part for his well-known concern for traffic hazards. Ironically, some sixteen months after MacDonald's hasty departure and Cox's equally abrupt arrival, on August 7, 1939, the partially completed Merritt Parkway suffered its first traffic fatality when eighteen-year-old Joseph V. Picone of Brooklyn dozed off at the wheel and struck the "rather nice" old oak, killing his uncle and passenger, Joseph Picone, instantly. It fell to Cox to investigate the fatality and determine the fate of the tree left standing by his predecessor. His initial response did not favor the junior Mr. Picone: "It seems to me," he observed, "that too many persons have passed the tree without incident to sustain the claim that the tree was the cause of the crash.... When a man falls asleep at the wheel, it is a matter of blind chance what he will hit." The New Canaan Garden Club also came to the tree's defense – again – when Myra Valantine, a member of the Club's executive committee, stated, "The tree is beautiful and should not be destroyed because of someone's carelessness." The oak conveniently showed signs of imminent mortality, presumably from old age, and was quietly and unceremoniously removed on January 30, 1940. The bend in the road was subsequently straightened.[9]

While the oak tree incident proved to be a tragic I-told-you-so event, some of Hurley's other charges against MacDonald were more substantial. In the area of mismanagement lay the whole Kemp land scam, which resulted not only in a prison sentence for Kemp but also in embarrassment for a number of highly visible public officials who had been feeding at the public trough. Stanley P. Mead of New Canaan, a Republican state assemblyman, judge of the New Canaan Town Court, chairman of the school board, and a member of the State Public Welfare Council, had, with a brother and sister, received a $100,000 payment for 28.1 acres of land assessed at $14,050.[10] As matters of public record, such transactions could hardly be disputed, and they led to reforms in the state's land acquisition policy in general, not just where the Merritt Parkway or other highways were concerned.

Instances of avarice in high places had a special poignancy given the still-depressed economy in the late 1930s. Of less popular interest but of greater long-term significance were Hurley's allegations concerning the technical aspects of the Merritt's design and construction. He pointed with a flourish to the potential danger of the "pinched bridges," characterizing the compression of traffic, particularly in underpasses, as a "death trap." He also condemned the overly sharp radius of curves on the road and on the exits and approaches to the parkway, as well as defects in construction – cracks in concrete bridges, poorly secured metal balustrades, and the like – that indicted Mac-Donald's oversight of construction.[11]

MacDonald rebutted these charges point by point as he had the oak tree matter, concluding that the fear of "death traps" was imaginary. The public wrangling between Hurley and MacDonald suggested a dangerous breakdown of authority in the administration of the highway program; as Governor Cross put it in his autobiography, "For months I had to placate two kings, as it were, sitting on the same throne." Cross called on the former highway commissioner and MacDonald's predecessor, Charles J. Bennett, to evaluate the conflicting claims. An engineer trained in an earlier time, Bennett supported most of the work on the Merritt, finding fault with only a few bridge designs. Bennett may have had greater reservations, but as Cross observed, "He was confronted . . . not with a theory but with the fact that fifty of the sixty bridges of the Parkway were already built or in the process of building. The cost of a radical change in their type would be prohibitive."[12]

Bennett clearly implied that most of Hurley's charges were without foundation, although the irony that the errors he did identify were literally cast in concrete was not lost on Hurley. The Bennett report did not silence Hurley, however, and to bolster his critique he cited no less an authority than Gilmore Clarke, whose Bronx River Parkway was the catalyst for the Merritt and many other highways of the period. In a 1937 lecture, "Interurban Traffic Problems," given at the Yale School of Fine Arts, Clarke had noted that the Merritt Parkway "may be said to be out of date before it is finished – as a matter of fact it was out of date before it was built."[13] He then listed some of the very shortcomings Hurley was pursuing. Later, when the Bennett review was made public,

Clarke, either by prior arrangement with Hurley or by pure serendipity – it is unclear which – voluntarily appeared in Cross's office to repeat his objections to the engineering of the Merritt. Cross chose Bennett's views, however, and so MacDonald continued the work as he had begun it. Only after Cox replaced MacDonald as highway commissioner later in 1938 were Hurley's criticisms, particularly of the pinched bridges, heeded. As a *Bridgeport Telegram* headline noted, "Lanes to Fan Out, Not Converge, on Parkway Bridge at Trumbull." [14]

**The Popular Response to the New Parkway**          Hurley and Clarke were not alone in their reservations about the parkway's merits, but the response of the public was nearly unanimous praise. The press might criticize the cupidity of Kemp and his associates, but its editorial comment was generous in its support. Editorial opinion spilled over into straight news coverage, with words like "beauty" and "graceful" and "impressive" used to describe the highway. One editorial writer waxed enthusiastic: "One can build a concrete highway anywhere. . . . But the Merritt parkway is different. More than any 'futurama' at the World's Fair, more than any dream of the futuristic designers, it shows what the highway of the future should really look like – a highway where the eye is filled with beauty and the mind with peace as the car purrs safely along." [15]

Nor was editorial praise limited to the local press. New York papers showed continuing interest in the progress of the new parkway. The Merritt tied into the Westchester County parkway system and so would allow easy access to Connecticut by New Yorkers, more and more of whom were moving there. And somehow the Merritt just seemed special. The *New York Herald-Tribune*, only weeks after the opening of the first segment of the road, ran the headline "Merritt Parkway Improves Upon Dreams of Its Best Advocates" and went on to observe, "The engineers have planned the route to provide travelers with opportunities to enjoy the varied beauties of the state." The report also emphasized that "real estate values have advanced before a demand for locations [justifying] the optimism of the leading men of Fairfield County." Further afield, Albert Wyss, writing in *Buick Magazine*, a General Motors publication sent to some six hundred thousand Buick owners, spoke of "the excellent job of balancing architectural considerations with engineering necessities" and predicting that it was "a good road to watch, for its safety features will soon be duplicated in your own locality." [16]

Letters to the editors also gauged the popular esteem in which the road and its builders were held. Many spoke of the beauties of nature that were enhanced by the new road;
others specifically came to MacDonald's defense when the brickbats started flying his
way. A *Bridgeport Post* reader called the unfinished parkway "a monument to the Late
John A. MacDonald," who had died in July 1938, several months after his resignation
and just weeks after the formal opening ceremonies in June. But no opinion weighed
more than that of the aged Schuyler Merritt. In a letter to Commissioner Cox in 1940, he
spoke glowingly of his now-completed namesake: "As I had nothing to do with its design or construction, I can without any immodesty praise heartily its beauty from every
point of view. I have long thought that the rural scenery of Connecticut was unexcelled
for beauty and a certain friendliness. I think the construction of the Parkway . . . does
not detract from this beauty, and in some ways adds to it." [17]

The attractiveness of the Connecticut countryside was not without its drawbacks,
however. The road attracted motorists unfamiliar with the novelty of a limited-access
highway who took too literally the *park* in *parkway*. Many drivers did not know how to
use it, although their misuse may be taken as a further measure of the highway's success. The Merritt Parkway Commission, which was finally empowered with the opening
of the first segment of the road, hurriedly passed a series of regulations to cope with
the abuses. Among the provisions a *Bridgeport Telegram* headline noted, "Parking —
and 'Sparking' – Banned on Parkway; Bridle Paths Undecided." [18] Proposed bridle paths
on the undeveloped 150 feet of the right-of-way were deferred after Attorney General
Charles McLaughlin ruled that Cox had no authority under existing law to build them.
(A system of horse trails was later developed but eventually abandoned.) On the other
hand, horses and buggies were clearly prohibited, as were trucks and commercial vehicles — a prohibition more honored in the breach in recent times. Also banned were
bicycles, pedestrians, billboards of any kind, and U-turns across the meridian, which
in those days had no barriers other than the curbing and grass strip. As an adjunct to
the parking ban, picnics were specifically ruled out: families on outings apparently had
taken to stopping along the way to avail themselves of the "park."

Schuyler Merritt, in his letter to Cox, addressed the matter of picnicking on the parkway. Although he agreed that there should be "no relaxation" of that ban, he wondered
if "city dwellers" might not be afforded the pleasure of an "occasional picnic" if it were
"practicable for the state to acquire about once in ten miles, a meadow or perhaps a

woodland which could be fixed up for a picnic ground... to give the rising generation a little chance for freedom and country air."

The ban on picnicking seems not to have been effectively enforced. The service plazas on the south side of the parkway had grassy areas on the unused portion of the right-of-way that were sometimes used for picnics. The continued presence of illegal picnickers and the Parkway Commission's proposal to establish an official picnic ground in Stamford provoked a hasty appeal for relief from one property owner to the governor. Harold Ross, the editor of *The New Yorker*, had built a colonial-style country retreat on eleven acres purchased from the sculptor Gutzon Borglum along the Rippowam River, within sight of the stone-veneered bridge Borglum had extorted from the state. Ross's objection to the proposed picnic area adjacent to his property grew out of experience: "Dozens of automobilists... stopped off, changed into and out of bathing suits in their cars, explored and overran the neighborhood, littered everything up with cans and papers, shouted and sang, swam in the little river there in their underwear or less, and committed the worst kind of nuisance in the stream, obnoxiously and dangerously polluting it."[19] Himself a weekday New Yorker, Ross concluded by echoing the fears voiced originally by Connecticut natives against the building of a parkway. "The parkway has put Stamford within 30 or 40 miles of... New York City and Stamford is sitting on a keg of dynamite.... I think you'd encourage a wave of petty thieving, and thieving not so petty, if you opened up the park." The picnic ground was never built.

If the Merritt had become an attractive nuisance in Ross's eyes, he was not alone in his apprehension about the effects of the parkway on both life-style and property values. Citizens in the town of Fairfield's remarkably affluent Greenfield Hill district had from the outset been among the most entrenched opponents to the parkway. Though they proved powerless to stop its construction or divert it around their enclave, they did forestall any interchanges from intruding on their tranquility.[20] This may have created a minor inconvenience for some of the residents who wanted ready access to the parkway, but it also insulated Greenfield Hill, they believed, from the onslaught of the dreaded New Yorkers. This xenophobia produced a still extant seven-and-a-half mile stretch without exits, the longest such segment on the Merritt, which is known to parkway mavens as "No-Man's Land." The political potency of the Greenfield Hill residents that prevented incursions was abetted, admittedly, by the state's obligation to build interchanges only for state surface highways, none of which crossed the parkway between Route 57 in Westport and Route 58 in Fairfield just beyond the Greenfield Hill boundary.[21] It was up to the towns to pay for additional interchanges if they wanted them, and Greenfield Hill property owners were able to convince Fairfield town fathers otherwise.

The sensitivity of the parkway's design, a chief objective of the FCPA, was universally applauded, but it was not the only feature so extolled. Two days after the first section of the road was opened, the *Bridgeport Telegram* proclaimed, "Parkway Saves 17 Minutes in Driving to New York City." With this route, the Hutchinson River Parkway, and Robert Moses's other New York parkways, it was now possible to drive the sixty-seven miles from Bridgeport to the Holland Tunnel in just two hours.[22] The reporter making the trip noted that the efficiency had to do with the lack of traffic lights. On the route from Bridgeport to the end of the Merritt, then in Norwalk, there were only thirty, and none on the parkways all the way to the Holland Tunnel. On the sixty-two mile return trip from New York via the old Boston Post Road there were 108 lights — more than three times as many — sixty-six of which the reporter hit on red! Clearly the objective of bypassing the traffic snarl on the Post Road had been realized.

**Additions & Alterations**        Before the second half of the parkway was finished, the original concept was already undergoing a transformation. The most obvious change was the introduction of tolls, which required legislative approval. And like most issues surrounding the parkway, the proposed pay-as-you-go plan was immediately controversial. Connecticut's long tradition of tolls — the Boston Post Road had been a toll road in part — had finally been eliminated early in the twentieth century when the newly organized State Highway Department took over the last of them. The toll roads had been privately owned, but their tolls were regulated by the legislature.[23] The idea that the state should become the toll collector did not sit well with many citizens who opposed the "driving tax" in principle: the Merritt was being built with a public bond issue to be retired by tax revenues, so to levy a road tax as well, they said, was clearly double taxation. Others, mainly commuters, who had already discovered the pleasures and efficiency of the half-finished Merritt, had a more obvious stake in opposing the tolls. And since the first toll station was planned for a site in Greenwich near the New York state line, still others feared that New York authorities might retaliate with a toll booth of their own, thus doubling the cost of using the new parkway route through Westchester County.

Who first proposed the new revenue measure seems to be one of the many lost details in the parkway's history. Highway Commissioner Cox was an early protagonist of the toll and enthusiastically imposed it once it was approved. The speed with which this was accomplished belies the canard that government operations inevitably move glacially. On June 6, in the closing hours of the 1939 legislative session, the senate approved an assembly bill authorizing the toll. Cox announced the next day that a temporary toll booth would be erected in Greenwich as soon as possible. Governor Raymond Baldwin (Wilbur Cross was defeated in his bid for a third term in 1938) signed the bill on the tenth, the signed bill was published on the fourteenth, and the first tolls were collected on June 21. The reason given for this astonishing speed was that the state was losing an estimated fifteen hundred dollars a day in revenue, a figure that proved conservative but was still substantial in the waning years of the Great Depression.[24]

Cox's alacrity in putting the temporary tolls in place was prompted by the impending Fourth of July holiday, when pleasure seekers were expected to stream through the toll station. William Grove, a traffic analyst for the Highway Department, had clocked some 16,300 cars just in the four-hour period from three to seven P.M. on Memorial Day and 31,000 on a typical Sunday in May.[25] Even at the authorized ten-cent toll, Cox found the prospects of collecting the booming Fourth of July tithe irresistible. In fact, the tolls poured in at a dizzying rate. On June 26, 24,757 cars paid tolls, and on July 23 — one month into toll collection — 30,480 dimes were deposited, bringing the first month's take to $61,142.90.[26]

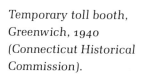

*Temporary toll booth, Greenwich, 1940 (Connecticut Historical Commission).*

Reactions to the toll were decidedly mixed. On June 22, the second day of the toll, Governor Baldwin drove to New York via the Merritt Parkway and dropped a dime in the money meter despite the exemption of state vehicles from paying tolls. He declared that he "never got as much value for any dime I ever spent," adding, "We in Connecticut believe in living within our means. That's what we are trying to do when we place a toll on the Merritt Parkway." Some drivers were less enthusiastic. On July 2, Matthew E. Scully of Union City, Connecticut, drove through the toll booth at thirty miles an hour and, according to the *Bridgeport Telegram* account, "hurled his dime at an attendant, the coin rolling off into the grass." Apprehended some three hundred feet from the toll booths by state troopers, Scully refused to get out of his car, creating a major traffic jam. His opinion of the toll resulted in his arrest for obstructing traffic.[27]

The idea of double taxation was a kind of red herring. From the outset the tolls were, by legislation, never intended to help pay for the Merritt but rather were earmarked for another project, the construction of an extension or continuation of the Merritt northward toward Hartford. This new road had already been dubbed the Wilbur Cross Parkway, not only in recognition of the efforts of the rejected former governor in getting the Merritt project built, but also for his service to the state in numerous other areas. It was presumably to this method of financing that Baldwin referred when he spoke of "living within our means." Other objections to the toll were quashed by pointing out that the drive was free if one only drove from the Housatonic River to Greenwich but did not drive into New York, or if one drove only from Greenwich into New York to get on the Hutchinson River Parkway. Both arguments seemed somewhat self-serving.

As for coping with the mountain of dimes that was piling up in the Greenwich toll house, the work was initially handled by assigned employees from the Highway Department. Permanent toll takers were subsequently hired, and the prospects must have been quite appealing: 140 applications were received to fill an anticipated twenty-three positions. Salaries in 1939 dollars ranged from $100 to $125 a month.[28]

Permanent toll booths were erected the next year. Designed by Dunkelberger, the structures were rustic log cabin–like wooden cubicles with the toll station – the offices – on the north side of the road. The toll barriers, always looking more temporary than permanent, proved quite fragile: badly aimed vehicles smashing into the booths resulted over the years in their virtual total piecemeal reconstruction. The Greenwich tolls finally were removed on June 25, 1988, at which time one section was sent to

*Permanent toll booth, Greenwich, c. 1942 (Department of Transportation, State of Connecticut).*

the Henry Ford Museum in Dearborn, Michigan, to become part of its huge exhibition on transportation in America.[29] At the same time the tolls were also removed from the Wilbur Cross Parkway; a section from the Housatonic bridge station was transferred to Boothe Memorial Park in Stratford.

Another change in the basic concept of the parkway concerned the commercial-use ban, as a call arose to allow service stations along the route. Cars of the period were not only less powerful than present models but were also prone to frequent mechanical failure and had a mysterious penchant for running out of gas. Lack of service stations on the Merritt or on the intersecting roads, which were mainly residential streets, left motorists stranded far from help in the event of a breakdown. State troopers who patrolled the parkway soon found that they were spending more time arranging for flat tires to be repaired or gas to be delivered to hapless drivers than they were dispensing speeding tickets. And the need for restrooms was hardly a lesser concern.

Cox proposed building service stations in pairs on either side of the parkway at three locations. Controversy immediately descended. Gas station operators as far away as the Post Road declared that their businesses would be ruined by the unfair competition of parkway stations, not realizing, apparently, that the parkway traffic was a captive clientele they would never tap anyway. Those few stations located on feeder roads – surface roads with interchanges at the parkway – probably did have a legitimate complaint, since their volume had increased markedly with the opening of the new route. Robert Gorham, a station operator on Main Street in Trumbull, reported that his business increased by three thousand dollars a year after the parkway opened.[30]

A more significant obstacle turned on a fine point of the law. Did the Highway Department have the legal authority to build gas stations? The attorney general's office ruled that the statute granting the highway commissioner authority to "erect either temporary or permanent buildings . . . for purposes incidental to the construction and maintenance of highways" applied to the Merritt Parkway since its design limited access to private filling stations.[31] This opinion, rendered on August 23, 1938, cleared the way for Cox and his staff to begin work on the stations, the first of which were erected in New Canaan near the South Street interchange. (A Highway Department maintenance yard adjacent to the station on the north lane was built concurrently.) Earl Wood, as engineer for roadside development, was in charge, and the architect again was George Dunkelberger. The plans for the New Canaan stations were approved by the Merritt Parkway Commission on February 28, 1939.[32] Construction began almost immediately, with the intention, Cox announced, of completing the work in time for the expected crowds traveling to the New York World's Fair that summer. The New Canaan stations did not open, however, until May 1940.

The fantasy and Art Deco brio that Dunkelberger brought to his earlier bridge designs seem to have eluded him this time, or, more probably, constraints were placed on him that had not previously been an impediment. In either event, his service stations are rather routine exercises in recycled colonial design, complete with red brick, white trim, and cupolas housing clocks.[33] Considering the exciting experimental filling-station designs being produced in these years, these conventional efforts are disappointing, however comfortably they might fit into the New England landscape of faux-colonial commercial buildings and motels. The notion that context demanded colonial stations ignored the solecism that there were no filling stations in colonial times; nor were there any colonial buildings, real or revivalist, along the parkway's rural route. Dunkelberger's inspiration may not have been so much contextual as borrowed. The Socony-Vacuum Oil Company (now the Mobil Oil Company) used colonial designs for its stations in the late 1920s and the 1930s, when it operated primarily in New York State and New England; streamlined, more or less Art Deco designs were introduced when the company went national.[34]

The mid-1930s, with its utopianism born of the Depression, found many architects studying urgent social problems. Frank Lloyd Wright characteristically addressed the whole fabric of the modern industrial society in his Broadacre City project, an integral component of which was a prototype filling station (Wright had an enduring love affair with high-performance cars). Others, like Walter Dorwin Teague and the Chicago firm Holabird and Root, took a less comprehensive approach to the city but produced dramatic filling-station designs that exploited the machine aesthetic of Art Deco. Some of these designs were sponsored by oil companies – Texaco in Teague's case[35] – which were attempting to upgrade the quality of their stations while polishing their corporate image. Dunkelberger's timid designs clearly represent a lost opportunity, but one guesses that exciting stations were not what the FCPA and its affiliates had in mind.

If the stations are not up to the design quality of the parkway itself, their operation under contract with the state was a model of what a service station should be, with the emphasis decidedly on service. Awarded in competitive bidding, the contracts stipulated that each station have a tow truck, that sales slips for emergency road work be issued to prevent price gouging, that the stations be open around the clock, that clean free restrooms be maintained at the lessee's expense, that the stations provide tire and minor repair services, and that a full line of gas and oil products be available.[36] The successful bidder paid a nominal rent for the station plus a royalty on each gallon of gas sold. This revenue went into the state highway fund and was used to pay for such recurring maintenance costs on the parkway as snow removal and grass mowing.[37]

The success of the New Canaan stations dictated the immediate construction of two more pairs, one in Greenwich just inside the Connecticut–New York state line, the other in Fairfield near the Sport Hill Road interchange, which were opened in the summer of 1941. An error on the side of conservatism – a problem that seemed to plague the parkway – was made in calculating the sales potential of the stations. Marketing experts estimated that the three pairs of stations together would pump one million gallons of gas a year, and the number of pumps and tank capacity as well as restrooms, parking spaces, and storage facilities were designed on the basis of this prediction. By fiscal year 1947 gas sales reached a remarkable five million gallons, requiring substantial remodeling of the service plazas. Traffic on the parkway had reached such volume that in just one month, July 1947, the parkway's service vehicles handled 583 emergency calls.[38] Traffic on weekends – the Saturday drive had come to compete with the traditional Sunday drive – often slowed to a crawl. One person recounted to me how, as a child, she would get out of the family car at the entrance to a service plaza, use the restroom, and catch up with the family again at the other end of the plaza!

Relocation of one stretch of the parkway also dates from the period after the opening of the first segment. The original plan called for the route to bend southward in Stratford to join the Boston Post Road at the Housatonic River. The success of the initial section of the parkway rekindled interest in casting a net of parkways across the state. The economic realities of the Depression had quashed this scheme earlier, but the idea of extending the Merritt northward to Hartford and the Massachusetts border seemed within reach. To this end, the Merritt was realigned to a point some three miles upstream, and a new high bridge with a span of 1,824 feet was constructed.

Technically the Merritt ends at the Housatonic and the Wilbur Cross begins on the other side. The bridge across the river, then, belongs to neither parkway, though it provides the vital link in the parkway system. The bridge's opening on September 2, 1940, marked the Merritt's official completion. But since it is not technically part of the Merritt, its cost – usually cited as $940,000 but sometimes given as $999,700 – is not included in the official total figure for building the Merritt, $22.7 million.[39]

One reason the cost of the bridge was kept below the original estimate of $1.5 million was the controversial use of an open steel grid for the road deck. The savings in weight (as opposed to a usual concrete roadbed) lowered the overall structural costs as well as the cost of the deck itself, and the speedup in the construction process also saved money. Like all compromises, however, it had its own costs. The surface causes a car to yaw, even at reasonable speeds. When wet, the deck, worn smooth by millions of miles of tires, can be dangerously slick, and in a winter freeze the bridge can be treacherous. Early users often detoured through Milford to the Post Road to avoid the bridge in the winter, although the Highway Department, not very convincingly, insisted that the heat of tires from passing cars would soon melt any ice buildup. Present-day drivers have generally made their peace with the quirky bridge, aided by more stable modern tire and suspension designs.

Since the bridge was part of neither parkway, it had to have a name of its own, and

*Housatonic River bridge from below steel grid deck.*

even that sparked a minor controversy. Several names historically attached to the area were promoted by various factions. Some wanted the bridge named for a local Revolutionary War hero, Major General David Wooster; others held out for Commodore Isaac Hull, a naval hero of the War of 1812. Some wanted it called the Oronoque, after the Native American name for the section of Stratford on the bridge's western (Merritt) terminus. Some even favored naming the bridge for Moses Wheeler, who ran the first ferry across the Housatonic in 1848. Backers of Hull maintained he had won a major naval victory over the British on the Housatonic River, but Wooster supporters proved that there never was such a battle and that their man, inter alia a Yale graduate, had documented ties to the area. The Native Americans, typically, were forgotten in the debate that ensued. Ultimately, none of these names was used for the bridge that drivers variously curse and avoid, but Hull's name was given to another Housatonic bridge on Route 8 north of the Merritt.[40]

A number of relatively minor alterations in use and structure were made to the Merritt Parkway soon after it was inaugurated. One was tied to what officials saw as an alarming rate of fatal accidents on the supposedly safe highway – a total of seven by the end of September 1940. The most notorious of these early accidents was not the first, the one involving Governor Cross's "rather nice" old oak tree, but one that occurred on July 21, 1940, leaving one person dead and eleven injured. Paul Solesbee of Mount Kisco, New York, who had never driven on the Merritt or, apparently, any other limited-access highway before, was heading for Westport and stopped for directions in Norwalk. Told to "take the first left" and get on the parkway, he did exactly that. Unfortunately, the first left took him onto an exit ramp, and he ended up driving into oncoming traffic; the Samaritan had neglected to tell Solesbee to cross the overpass before turning. Solesbee managed to avoid one car but hit the next, driven by Ernest Tremblay of Willimantic, head on.

The county coroner exonerated Solesbee since the small sign marking the exit had been knocked down some time earlier and had not been replaced.[41] This incident led to rethinking the attitude toward signs on the parkway. Originally, in the spirit of preventing commercial intrusions on the natural setting of the Merritt, signs were deliberately kept to a minimum and made small and unobtrusive. This environmental concern and the novelty of a divided highway were not compatible, and signs along the Merritt have grown in number and size ever since. It was in this context that the blue and white Merritt Parkway shields, based on the state seal and intended to direct drivers to the parkway from the back roads, were introduced on March 16, 1945. They are still in use, although many are battered and others have fallen prey to graffiti artists.

Another change motivated by the soaring accident rate was the speed limit. Originally set at fifty miles an hour in the daytime and forty at night, the State Traffic Commission ordered the speed lowered to forty miles an hour at all times. The result of the speed reduction, which took effect on January 10, 1942, was an immediate 40 percent drop in the accident rate, or so the *Bridgeport Post* contended. Reportable accidents from December 10 through January 9 had been forty-seven; for the period ending February 9, the figure had dropped to twenty-eight.[42] A sixty-day survey seems inadequate proof to substantiate such a radical reduction, however.

Excessive speed seems to have been a problem on the parkway from the beginning. Several responses were tried in the early years besides the speed reduction, whose efficacy was at best inconclusive. That speed limits were subsequently raised, then lowered and raised yet again, suggests some uncertainty in Hartford as to whether to come down on the side of safety or efficiency. The need for special law enforcement as well as some means of aiding stranded motorists had already been recognized when a detail of twelve state highway troopers was assigned fulltime to the parkway, with a barracks projected for the same location as the westbound service station in New Canaan. (It was never built.) Effective January 8, 1941, they were given their own supervising sergeant, John Hanusovsky, who had served as the personal chauffeur to Governor Raymond Baldwin until that date, when Baldwin, who had lost his bid for reelection, was replaced as governor by Robert Hurley.[43]

It is unclear how much the tickets they dispensed served to maintain speed limits. To judge from press reports of continuing speeding problems, the answer is: not much. To contain speeders' natural urges, in the late 1940s, especially on Sundays and holidays, pairs of state patrol cars would drive abreast down the parkway at or below the speed limit, effectively escorting a swelling parade of vehicles the length of the parkway. No record of when or why this practice was discontinued seems to exist. The New Jersey state police, who experimented with this traffic control device in the late 1980s on the New Jersey Turnpike and the Garden State Parkway, cited decreasing traffic flow and increasing driver frustration as the reasons they abandoned the program.

Other significant changes in use patterns occurred with the advent of World War II and gas rationing. Traffic volume dropped dramatically as measured at the toll booths: according to the *Bridgeport Post*, parkway traffic decreased a remarkable 83 percent from its prewar level by January 1943. Simultaneously, women replaced drafted men as toll takers, and even more significantly, in a reversal of established policy, the Merritt Parkway Commission, as a contribution to the war effort, voted to allow trucks carrying war materiel to use the nearly deserted road beginning June 15, 1943. Since explosives were banned from the Boston Post Road because of the heavily populated towns along its route, the Merritt made an important contribution to the military effort. Truck traffic was quickly suspended at war's end. On August 18, 1945, just four days after the Japanese surrender, the Parkway Commission reinstated the suspension as part of the postwar "measures to protect the homefront from traffic casualties." The commission no doubt had in mind a disastrous accident that occurred on June 15, 1945: four persons were killed when their car crashed into a navy truck parked on the fog-shrouded parkway.[44]

This period also saw a number of other firsts. Starting May 3, 1947, the State Highway Commission – not the Merritt Parkway Commission – ordered the numbering of the exits, which had been known simply by the name of the cross street. The policy was

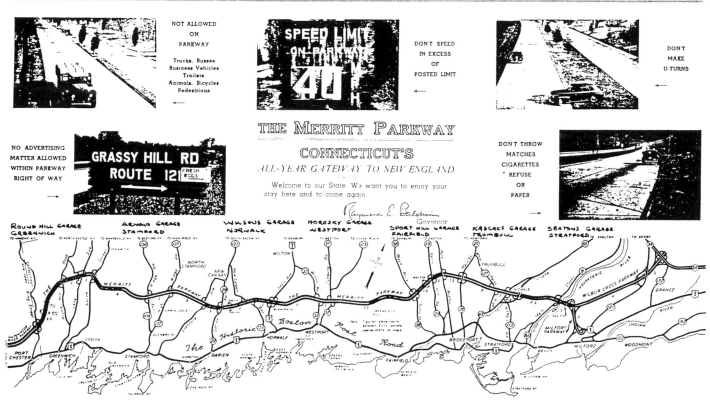

OBEY THESE RULES OF THE MERRITT PARKWAY COMMISSION

NOT ALLOWED
ON
PARKWAY

Trucks. Busses
Business Vehicles
Trailers
Animals. Bicycles
Pedestrians

SPEED LIMIT ON PARKWAY 40 M.P.H.

DON'T SPEED
IN EXCESS
OF
POSTED LIMIT

DON'T
MAKE
U-TURNS

NO ADVERTISING
MATTER ALLOWED
WITHIN PARKWAY
RIGHT OF WAY

GRASSY HILL RD ROUTE 121 FRESH EGGS

THE MERRITT PARKWAY
CONNECTICUT'S
ALL-YEAR GATEWAY TO NEW ENGLAND

Welcome to our State. We want you to enjoy your
stay here and to come again.

*Raymond E. Baldwin*
Governor

DON'T THROW
MATCHES
CIGARETTES
REFUSE
OR
PAPER

*Informational brochure handed out at Merritt Parkway toll booths, c. 1948–50 (New Canaan Historical Society).*

apparently in response to the numerous accidents, mostly minor, that resulted from strangers slowing down while trying to identify their intended exits. The small, rustic wooden signs initially installed along the parkway have long ago given way to standard green and white billboard-sized placards. To further orient newcomers to the Merritt, the toll takers began handing out small brochures with a schematic map of the route, a friendly note of welcome to the parkway (this time from the Merritt Commissioners), and a less friendly list of dos and don'ts for the novice driver.

One of the more notorious firsts was the first violent crime on the Merritt Parkway, committed on September 25, 1945. Martin Hessekiel, a wholesale fur salesman from

New York, was robbed of thirteen thousand dollars in furs plus $104 in cash after being stopped on the parkway, then bound, gagged, and beaten near the Congress Street overpass in the town of Fairfield. The culprits apparently were never apprehended.[45]

The first violation of the noncommercial status of the parkway had occurred even before the entire route opened. Baldemero Piro, twenty, of White Plains, New York, was arrested in Stamford for driving a truckload of furniture on the parkway on November 16, 1939. That he had to post a $75 bond for the infraction in those late Depression days suggests how seriously the injunction on commercial traffic was then taken.[46] Today, pickup trucks loaded with home appliances, ladders, and other commercial wares ply the Merritt with seeming impunity, much to the consternation of commuters, who conveniently forget that the road was never intended for commuting, either. The only trucks that today seem to run afoul of the law are occasional large semitrailers, usually moving vans, that wander onto the parkway but get stalled at the first overpass. Backing the behemoths off the parkway is presumably as humiliating for the hapless drivers as it is inconvenient for motorists whose cars queue up for miles behind the immobilized trucks.

The goal of keeping commercial development off parkway land has been much more successful. There was one effort (aside from the service plazas) to breach this ban, however. In 1940, Austin Mather proposed the construction of a "Colonial Village" to be part museum, part showcase for Connecticut manufactured goods. The plan called for a cluster of ersatz colonial buildings not unlike the filling stations then going up along the parkway; they were to be built on state-owned land in Greenwich near the beginning of the Merritt. The plan apparently gained the support of the Fairfield County Planning Association, the arch enemy of anything that smacked of commercialism, but the proposal, like so many others, became a casualty of World War II.[47]

Another proposal for a museum was made the following year, lay dormant during the war, and was resurrected in 1945. The tenor James Melton, a Weston resident and the popular star of such radio programs as "Harvest of Stars" and "The Telephone Hour," offered to donate his collection of antique automobiles to a museum to be built on a site accessible from the parkway. The project actually made it through the state legislature — in fact more easily than the parkway itself had originally been authorized. One hundred and fifty thousand dollars was appropriated for the construction of the museum, the funds to be repaid by admission fees. That Melton was chairman of the Merritt Parkway

Commission and had strong allies in the legislature helped gain the approval, but the popular outcry against the museum proved more potent than Melton's support in Hartford, and this project too was soon dropped. One irate reader wrote to the *Bridgeport Post* that Melton's proposed gift would turn the parkway into a "junk yard." Many in Fairfield County seemed to agree, feeling that the tenor had been singing a self-serving song to the legislature.[48] Eventually, Melton's collection found a home, far from the Merritt Parkway, in a museum in Sarasota, Florida.

Building the parkway had incurred a bonded debt to the state of Connecticut. On November 20, 1940, Highway Commissioner Cox disclosed in his biennial report that the Merritt Parkway had paid its first "dividend" to the state – $493,439 from tolls collected at the Greenwich toll house. Actually, by that time the Highway Department had already paid $926,940 in interest and $3,432,000 in principal on the bonds, all of it taken from the department's regular budget. Cox also disclosed the final official cost of the Merritt: $20,592,001.31, exclusive of interest on the bonds, which came to a further $2,100,000. Of the capital expenditure figure, $11.1 million was for construction, $6.9 million for land acquisition, $1.6 million for landscaping – well above MacDonald's projected allotment of $250,000 – and $856,368 on engineering expenses.[49] Because the bonds were retired with the Highway Department's regular funds, claiming that a "dividend" from the tolls was paying for the parkway was incorrect, if not intentionally deceptive: Cox knew, of course, that the tolls were being used to build the Wilbur Cross Parkway.

The Merritt Parkway that came into being was remarkably close to what Schuyler Merritt and the FCPA advocates had hoped it would be. It provided a safe and efficient alternative to the Boston Post Road without sacrificing the beauty of the countryside it crossed. A report issued by the Merritt Parkway Commission in May 1946 compared the accident rates of the Merritt and the Post Road for the period from January 1, 1940, to January 1, 1945.[50] The Post Road had experienced 4,059 accidents, more than three times the number on the Merritt (1,250), although it carried not even twice as much traffic (920 million vehicle miles to the parkway's 563 million). Almost five times as many people died in crashes on the Post Road (97) as on the Merritt (21).

By 1947, traffic on the Merritt Parkway had returned to prewar levels. On Memorial Day of that year, 38,175 cars passed through the Greenwich tolls – this before Detroit had completed retooling from war production. The home construction industry was even slower to recover from wartime priorities. When it did, it faced a pent-up demand for housing caused by the Depression hiatus in home building as well as the return of millions of G.I.s intent on establishing families. Most new housing was constructed on the periphery of existing towns, but with the corporate limits of cities fixed, development soon spilled over into unincorporated countryside. Thus the pre-Depression trickle of families leaving the cities for the suburbs now became, after World War II, the flood of suburbanization that contributed to the virtual destruction of the nation's cities. The effects on the nation's highways were similarly calamitous.

The Merritt was hardly immune to the traffic snarls that became the norm everywhere. And, as elsewhere, little more than hand wringing was the public response. The problem was compounded at the Merritt by a smug satisfaction that the highway, completed only a decade earlier, was still a thing of beauty which was never intended to carry the loads now demanded of it by commuters. The once pastoral parkway had begun to resemble a parking lot during rush hours, and its serenity was broken by the blasting horns of frustrated motorists.

The increase in traffic was complicated by another unforeseen development. The gleaming white concrete road surface began to deteriorate at an alarming rate. Surface spalling or chipping quickly gave way to cracking and then to yawning potholes. At the time the Merritt's roadway was laid, there had been relatively little progress in concrete technology since the first modern concrete street was paved in 1893 in Bellefontaine, Ohio.[51] In the 1930s, contractors typically used far more water than was needed to turn cement into concrete, the so-called water of hydration. The excess water made a more easily worked mix, but it also weakened the finished concrete – thus the spalling. Current practice calls for an engineer to make a "slump test" on each batch of wet concrete before it is poured to insure that too much water is not used.

The heavy pounding of automobile traffic and the wartime truck traffic undoubtedly took a toll on the Merritt's already weakened surface. (Heavy traffic, especially trucks, have had similar deleterious impact on the postwar Interstate System.) And the use of salt on the roadway in winter attacked not only the ice but also the surface itself through chemical action with the lime in the concrete. This same process ate away, more slowly, at the bridges and their balustrades as the result of seepage from the melting salty ice and from salt splash.

The answer to the breakdown of the surface was a coat of blacktop. The *Bridgeport*

*Post* reported the problem as early as 1947, and on May 24, 1949, the first section of the parkway was given a hot asphalt treatment in the Greenwich area.[52] The dual bands of white soon turned black from one end of the parkway to the other. Repeated applications over the years destroyed another novel feature of the roadway: the glass reflectors set in the concrete curbs. They were buried under layers of asphalt, and so the parkway lost one of its much-touted innovative safety features.

**The Wilbur Cross Extension & Interstate 95**       With the end of the world war, construction resumed on the Wilbur Cross Parkway, the technically separate continuation of the Merritt northward past New Haven and on to Hartford via the Berlin Turnpike. Although the Wilbur Cross is not part of the Merritt, its story helps put the Merritt's in perspective. And since the Wilbur Cross was built with funds generated by the Merritt tolls, it may quite properly be thought of as the child of the Merritt. Because many of the same hands were involved in both projects, comparisons are inevitable.

*Decay of concrete, Grumman Avenue overpass, Westport.*

The idea in the 1930s for a new route paralleling the Boston Post Road through Fairfield County soon led to an ambitious proposal for a network of parkways crisscrossing Connecticut. The plan was never realized, but the idea of extending the new road to Hartford did gain support almost from the beginning. Enthusiasm was especially strong in the Yale University community and in New Haven because of academic and other connections with New York City. New Haven had long marked the outer limits of commuter train service, so it was inevitable that pressure would build for a link with the new Merritt road, which ended some fifteen miles to the west of the city. This demand, along with the desire in southwest Connecticut for a faster route to Hartford (strongly supported by many Fairfield County legislators) was met with the omnibus bill that the state legislature passed on June 6, 1939, mandating that tolls be collected on the Merritt to fund the extension. Planning apparently had already begun, and construction started the next year. The imposition of wartime materiel restrictions practically halted the project, however, and it was not until after the war that work was pursued again in earnest.

The completed Wilbur Cross Parkway runs from the Commodore Hull Bridge in Milford to the Berlin Turnpike in Meriden (where it now merges into Interstate 91), a distance of about twenty-nine miles. The highway consists of two twenty-four-foot con-

*West Rock tunnel, Wilbur*
*Cross Parkway, Woodbridge.*

crete lanes with a nominal twenty-foot landscaped median as opposed to the twenty-six-foot lanes and twenty-two-foot median on the Merritt, and it has forty-three grade separations to the Merritt's sixty-eight. Because of its shorter length (the Merritt covers 37.5 miles) and narrower roadbed, the total cost for construction and land acquisition was also lower: $17.5 million against $22.7 million. The Wilbur Cross has one feature not found on the Merritt – a twin tunnel through the red sandstone West Rock ridge at Woodbridge.

These statistics do little, however, to explain why motorists feel an affection for the Merritt that does not seem to extend to the Wilbur Cross – or at least not in the same degree. One major difference stems from the topography of the two routes. The rolling landscape that animates the Merritt is largely absent on the other side of the Housatonic River. There are a few hilly sections with pleasant vistas on the stretch up to the West Rock tunnel, but from that point the route cuts inland toward Hartford, where the terrain flattens out. North from New Haven the road is often as straight as the railroad configuration Schuyler Merritt feared for his namesake. Further, the Wilbur Cross is a more urban road than its rural counterpart in Fairfield County. The section that extends from Woodbridge through New Haven and Hamden to North Haven is especially urbanized. Industrial parks, motels, and shopping centers crowd the parkway with little or none of the protective greenbelt that generally masks such developments along the Merritt, even the recent intensive commercialization in Stamford and at the Route 7 interchange in Norwalk.

The design of the Wilbur Cross seems less inspired than that of the Merritt. This is hard to explain since several members of the original Merritt team were in charge of designing the Wilbur Cross. Earl Wood once again headed up landscaping and roadside development, with Thayer Chase as his designer. Where the setting is still substantially rural, as in Orange, they worked their usual magic, but the more urban stretches around New Haven or the flat area around Wallingford and Meriden offered neither the opportunity nor the inspiration for the kind of work that is typical of the Merritt. The result is a perfectly pleasant road that still deserves to be called a parkway, but it is no Merritt.

Even more disappointing is the lackluster work of George Dunkelberger, who rehearsed his role as bridge architect. Those bridges built before the war in Milford and Orange as a direct extension of his work on the Merritt do show the same spirit that informs the earlier designs. The Route 34 overpass, for example, would not look out of place on the Merritt, although the rather badly underscaled heraldic shields – the coats of arms of Orange and Yale University – that ornament the crowns of the segmental arches are symptomatic of the anemic designs he produced for the Wilbur Cross. Dunkelberger continued on as a regular (rather than WPA) employee of the Highway Department after the war, but the bridges designed in that period are plain to the point of being undistinguished. Gone are the bold touches of inspired whimsy that characterized his best work – the Nike wings on the James Farm Road overpass, for example. Even the classicizing elegance of the more traditional bridges seems to have eluded him in the later stretches of the Wilbur Cross, many of which look as if the engineer's functionalism had completely overridden the architect's art.

Why the Wilbur Cross did not live up to the standards of its predecessor remains an open question. The budgets were not significantly different, and in any event the Merritt tolls guaranteed adequate funding. Part of the decline of the postwar work may be attributable to the austerity right after the war, when shortages were the order of the day. Moreover, the often whimsical aspect of Art Deco that Dunkelberger had exploited before the war so effectively seemed out of touch with a world overshadowed by the

*Stone-veneered underpass, Wilbur Cross Parkway.*

*Route 121 overpass, Wilbur Cross Parkway, Orange.*

*Bishop Street overpass, Wilbur Cross Parkway, North Haven, c. 1950 (Department of Transportation, State of Connecticut).*

carnage of the war, the Holocaust, and the atomic bomb. At the same time, the ascendancy of the no-nonsense "functionalism" of the Bauhaus was a direct assault on Art Deco designs, which the functionalists labeled frivolous and trivial.[53] Bauhaus bashing, popularized by Tom Wolfe in his *From Bauhaus to Our House*, is an obsessive pastime of postmodern criticism, which often ignores the real contributions of Walter Gropius and his colleagues. Yet it does seem likely that a certain blandness that replaced the exuberance of Art Deco following the war stemmed from the tenets of the International Style fostered by Gropius at Harvard's Graduate School of Design, to which he had been appointed in 1937. Dunkelberger did not make the trek to Harvard as many younger architecture students on the G.I. Bill did following the war; but he had a history of accommodating design fads and would undoubtedly have been aware of Gropius's work and ideas from their exposure in the professional press. This combination of external forces and his own lack of a design commitment may account for the direction his work on the Wilbur Cross took. Or perhaps, more simply, he had spent his creative resources on the earlier Merritt designs.

In one respect there was common ground between the two parkways. Late in 1941, the *Bridgeport Sunday Herald* revealed that "the ghosts of the Merritt Parkway scandal are on the prowl again."[54] But unlike the Kemp land scam, in the case of the Wilbur Cross the graft was within the Highway Department itself. The *Sunday Herald* leveled charges of misappropriation of construction funds, misuse of state equipment, double dipping on the part of Highway Department employees (who billed private contractors for work already paid for by the state, thus effectively billing the state twice), as well as "a mass of peculiar incidents, mainly of petty chiseling." William Cox, who had replaced John MacDonald as highway commissioner after Kemp's activities became public, now found himself in deep legal trouble and was later removed from office.

By the 1960s another new highway was also affecting the life of the Merritt. Interstate 95, now the principal route from Maine to Florida, was part of the original system projected by the National Interstate and Defense Highway Act of 1944 funded by Congress, finally, in 1956. The Connecticut portion, which parallels Long Island Sound and the Boston Post Road, was dedicated on January 2, 1958. Much more ambitious than the Merritt Parkway, it is 129 miles long, has 247 bridges and 90 interchanges, and cost $464 million, more than twenty times as much as the parkway.[55] In terms of design, it is closer to the later phases of the Wilbur Cross, lacking the scenic attributes of the

Merritt. But I-95 did for trucks what the Merritt had done earlier for cars, by providing an alternative to the clogged main streets of the shore towns. It also helped relieve the ever-growing congestion on the parkway itself since it offered a faster if less scenic route for commuters driving to New York.

The relief proved temporary, however, again confirming the Moses axiom that traffic increases to fill the highway space available to it. In the mid-1950s, traffic on the Merritt averaged thirty-two thousand vehicles a day; in 1960, after the opening of I-95, the figure dropped to about twenty thousand a day. By 1980, however, the congestion had returned to the thirty-thousand range and was rising. Although the population of towns along the Merritt did not increase dramatically in that period, car ownership did. Between 1970 and 1985 in Trumbull, for example, a town abutting Bridgeport, the population rose by only a thousand people, or about 3 percent. But car ownership jumped from about eighteen thousand to about twenty-seven thousand – a 50 percent increase.[56]

**The DOT versus the Merritt Parkway**          The rebounding of traffic on the Merritt led the Highway Department, rebaptized the Department of Transportation (DOT), to turn its attention to the parkway with the idea of improving it. Some of its efforts in the 1970s and 1980s were clearly helpful. One of the principal causes of accidents was the tight entrances and exits and the related lack of acceleration and deceleration lanes. Department of Transportation engineers have corrected these flaws at a number of interchanges (though not all of them), making the parkway safer and more efficient without seriously compromising the original design.

Other "improvements" have been less salubrious. The unobtrusive (and ineffective) post-and-rail barriers that originally guarded steep fills and many of the interchanges gave way first to heavier posts and steel cables, which were still fairly rustic. Then the posts were replaced with steel stanchions, and recently the cables were removed in favor of the galvanized ribbed steel "rails" commonly used on the interstate highways. Again, this change has certainly improved safety, but at a visual cost. The new steel rails run down the median strip as well as along most of the outer edge of the parkway, and at overpasses and underpasses they are generally stacked two high, creating a tunnel effect that blocks the view of parts of Dunkelberger's bridges. Purists among parkway users see these intrusive features as unwelcome gifts of insensitive DOT engineers.

Post and rail barrier, near
North Street, Greenwich
(Department of Transportation, State of Connecticut).
**top left**

Post and cable, near Frenchtown Road, Trumbull
(Department of Transportation, State of Connecticut).
**top right**

Ribbed galvanized-steel
guard.

More disturbing has been the shoddy repair and maintenance of the parkway. Budgetary constraints have generally been cited for the demise of the landscaping. Admittedly, the blame does not lie entirely with the DOT in this case. A combination of calamities has drastically altered Thayer Chase's careful plantings, including winter salt runoff, pollution from the lead and acidic emissions of modern high-compression automobile engines, natural depredations such as Dutch elm disease, and the death of trees either from simple old age and the invasion of nonnative plants like the Oriental bittersweet, a climbing vine that now shrouds much of the roadside. Some of these problems could have been prevented; others could have been corrected by new plantings of disease- or pollution-resistant strains. Little has been done, however, beyond removing the trees that have died, which now include nearly all of the mountain laurel (the state flower) and the dogwoods, which had made the Merritt drive as spectacular in the spring as the brilliant autumn colors do in the fall.[57] Even the conifers have been subject to this neglect, so that the drive along the parkway today is radically different from what it was even twenty years ago. Thayer Chase, who had not driven on the Merritt in several decades, revisited the parkway in the summer of 1991. "T'ain't what it used to be," he commented, especially saddened by the loss of the laurels and the trees planted in the median strip that had contributed so much to the leafy canopy.[58]

*Landscaping and bridge abutment overrun by Oriental bittersweet, Round Hill Road overpass, Greenwich.*

Unfortunately, the DOT's laissez-faire stewardship has extended to the bridges on the parkway as well. Failure to perform preventive maintenance against damage from the salting of roads and the aging of the concrete has resulted in the serious deterioration of many bridges. Some have needed to have the original spalled-concrete surface removed and a new surface troweled on the bridges in the manner of icing a cake. In others the spans became structurally unsound and had to be completely removed to the abutments and rebuilt along the lines of the original design. Although these late – even too late – preservation efforts are admirable for attempting to perpetuate the original parkway concept, in practice the DOT's actions have permanently altered the appearance of the bridges. The elimination of detail and the use of an epoxy resin sealant have destroyed Dunkelberger's carefully selected color schemes and pebbly, exposed aggregate surfaces; the glint of quartz has been replaced by a grayish-white sepulchral cast. These rebuilt bridges stand out from the landscape instead of blending in with it. Elsewhere, as at the Morehouse Highway overpass, repairs have been made so crudely as to all but ruin the effect of the design. These are stark reminders of how fragile these works of art are and how easily they may be permanently disfigured when entrusted to well-meaning but insensitive hands.

*Rebuilding the Marvin Ridge Road overpass, New Canaan, 1990.*

The DOT has also been responsible for alterations to the parkway that go beyond cosmetic tampering. In the late 1970s, plans were developed to turn state routes 8 and 25 into freeways to ease traffic congestion running northerly out of Bridgeport. The result is a series of massive high-speed interchanges with the Merritt in Trumbull. Gone are the Merritt's traditional close encounters with nature. The Trumbull interchanges sprawl over acres of land where the Connecticut forest, which once overhung the parkway like a cathedral vault, was leveled. At such places the parkway looks hardly different from any interstate highway.

Trumbull residents, suspicious of the DOT's intentions from the outset, railed against plans to alter or destroy the bridges in the path of this dubious progress. Ironically, the fervor of this defense of the parkway matched the zeal of the local opposition to its construction fifty years earlier. But whereas the landed gentry of Greenfield Hill in Fairfield had in the 1930s prevented any kind of interchange in their neighborhood, producing the seven-and-a-half-mile exitless "no-man's land," the Trumbull protesters were less successful in their cause. The DOT kept reassuring the public that its plans would have a minimal impact on the parkway. Karl Crawford, the chief engineer for the DOT, an-

*Painting the Stanwich Road overpass, Greenwich, with white epoxy sealant, 1991.*

*These two views of the Morehouse Highway overpass before (**left**) and after (**right**) the 1990 repairs show the loss of subtle detail in Dunkelberger's triple-faceted arches.*

*Connecticut Route 25 interchange, Trumbull.*

swering a letter protesting the removal of several of the original bridges, stated "that all viable alternatives have been considered and that the design selected [for the new interchanges] will provide an acceptable level of service with the least impact on the Merritt Parkway, its bridges and the surrounding environment."[59]

Despite Crawford's avowal, the resulting seven bridges that crisscross the parkway with long-span steel box trusses clearly do "impact" on the original design. These new overpasses are actually quite handsome and would, with their sweeping forms, be a visual asset on an interstate freeway. But on the Merritt they are an intrusion, an interruption in the serene unity of the parkway's original conception. Several existing bridges underwent major alterations, and two, the Route 8 overpass and the Huntington Turnpike (Route 108) underpass, were totally demolished "due to a reversal of the over-under relationship of the Parkway and the intersecting roads," as Crawford put it.[60] As a sop to the local supporters of the parkway and in the spirit of historic preservation, the DOT salvaged some of the cast-iron ornament from the Huntington bridge and pasted it like so much wallpaper on the new bridge's abutments.

Fear of such assaults on the parkway and the DOT's periodic talk of widening sections of the road had already galvanized concerned users into a citizens' action group. Founded in 1973, the Save the Merritt Association was one of the many protest movements that seemed to have sprung up in the wake of the Vietnam War as the apathy

*Route 8 overpass, Trumbull.*

*Huntington Turnpike over-pass, Trumbull, with remnants of ornament from the original bridge.*

and noninvolvement of earlier decades were replaced with activism, including the rise of the environmental movement and the preservation efforts. In 1976, it was joined by a quasi-official body, the Merritt Parkway Advisory Committee, whose function it was to "advise" the DOT on matters affecting the parkway. That the two groups had overlapping memberships – Joan Caldwell of Greenwich, a concerned citizen appalled by the DOT's plans for the parkway, was a founder of the one and a member of the other – made for coordinated but largely unsuccessful preservation efforts. Thus, the Route 8/Route 25 debacle appears to be repeating itself in the immense new interchange for the upgraded U.S. Route 7 now being constructed in Norwalk.

*"Super 7" interchange,
Norwalk, 1992.*

Another group, the Northwest Greenwich Association, led again by Caldwell, was
the moving force behind the effort in 1974–75 to have the parkway placed on the
National Register of Historic Places. Although the National Register does not insure
preservation of listed sites, it does encourage it and can considerably delay any proposed demolition through protracted appeals. The nomination sailed through the elaborate approval process, gaining endorsement finally from the Connecticut Historical
Commission, only to be rejected by Governor Ella Grasso, apparently on the advice of
DOT officials who feared such listing might prevent their planned "improvements" and
alterations of the road.

The fears of Caldwell and her associates proved to be well founded when the DOT
announced its ambitious plans for the parkway in a March 1990 preliminary report
entitled "Southern Connecticut Transportation Corridor Study: Transit Strategies and
Highway Concepts." The plan projected demographic data through the year 2010 and
suggested that Interstate 95 be expanded to twelve lanes from the present six. More
ominous were the projections for the Merritt.

One alternative would expand the existing road from four to six lanes. This would
mean the loss of the seven double-arched overpasses with central supports and an un-
told sacrifice of underpasses that would have to be widened. A more radical alternative,
the "Full Build Eight Lanes" plan, would convert the parkway to an eight-lane route

with the construction of a mirror-image roadway on the unused 150-foot portion of the original 300-foot right-of-way. This scheme would allegedly leave the present roadway intact as the westbound four lanes with the new parallel four lanes serving eastbound traffic. But it would mean the virtual destruction of the greenbelt that is an integral part of the parkway. The DOT engineers, whose plans seem to ignore mass transit as a solution, have made much of the fact that this reserved right-of-way was always intended to serve future expansion, but they seem disarmingly unaware that it has since become a buffer between the parkway and the hundreds of houses that have been built along its perimeter in the postwar years. Moreover, the ample experience of other highway expansions shows that an expanded Merritt Parkway would surely become as snarled with traffic as the present route is today. Much would be lost, and little gained.

Fortunately, alert and aggressive defenders of the parkway's integrity came forward to challenge the DOT. The Connecticut Trust for Historic Preservation, a citizen action group dedicated to saving the historic built environment from destruction by either private developers or public agencies, again sought official recognition for the parkway by renominating it for the National Register. With the generous financial support of Rene Anselmo of Greenwich,[61] chairman of the Pan American Satellite Corporation, the trust was able to move quickly in preparing the nomination documents before the DOT's plans could be advanced. Support for the renewed nomination effort came from many quarters. John W. Shannahan, the state's historic preservation officer and director of the Connecticut Historical Commission, declared: "We need to give the Parkway the legitimate recognition that it has long deserved. . . . By writing this nomination . . . we can make the case for the national significance of the parkway. Then . . . we will be making decisions about the Merritt Parkway with the full knowledge of what we have and why it is so special."[62] This time the nomination was successful: on April 17, 1991, the Merritt was officially listed on the National Register with the blessing of Governor Lowell Weicker. What effect this will have on the DOT proposal to "improve" the parkway is impossible to say, but it seems certain that the Connecticut Trust and other concerned groups will be carefully monitoring the DOT and using the Merritt's new status to preserve what remains of this national treasure.

Meanwhile, in the summer of 1991, a documentation team from the National Trust in Washington spent six weeks studying the Merritt, producing measured drawings of a representative selection of the bridges, taking thousands of photographs of all the bridges and general views of the parkway, and attempting to reconstruct the original landscaping scheme. This extensive documentation will further help preserve this part of our patrimony.

# THE
# MERRITT
# PARKWAY'S
# LONG
# SHADOW

The completion of the Merritt Parkway occurred at a pivotal moment, just when the United States was pulling out of the Great Depression and was being drawn into the war in Europe and Asia. In 1940, Americans remained amazingly innocent of the events in Europe while enjoying a measure of economic recovery at home. If the times were not easy, at least they were easier than they had been for a decade. Gasoline sold for under twenty cents a gallon, and people took to the roads in droves. By the end of the 1930s they had roads to drive on that were designed for cars, not carriages, and the Merritt was among the finest.

The Merritt was not the only new superhighway, however. The first section of Hitler's Autobahn, opened near Frankfurt in 1935, was more advanced than most highways in the United States, with its use of limited access, median strips, and landscaping.[1] In 1933 Chicago's Lakeshore Drive debuted, speeding traffic southward from the congested downtown Loop area (later the route was extended along the northern lake front as well). In San Francisco, the Golden Gate Bridge, with its parkway-like approach roads, opened with great festivities in 1937. Just a month after the opening of the Housatonic River bridge marked the official completion of the Merritt, the Pennsylvania Turnpike was opened to traffic on October 1, 1940. Both roads, in different ways, celebrated America's love affair with the automobile and showed that Norman Bel Geddes's futuristic image of "Magic Motorways," featured in the General Motors pavilion at the 1939 New York World's Fair, was more than a visionary's fantasy.[2]

The differences between the two highways are fundamental. The 160-mile Pennsylvania Turnpike was intended as a fast link between Pittsburgh and Harrisburg, the state capital. (The turnpike was extended after the war to Philadelphia and was connected by bridge to the New Jersey Turnpike.) In name and concept, Pennsylvania built a road derived from the private toll roads of the eighteenth and nineteenth centuries. The new turnpike, incorporating the new engineering concepts of grade separations and median strips to separate opposing lanes of traffic, was designed to move traffic as directly and efficiently as possible from point A to point B. Trucks and buses were not only welcome but were also key to its economic viability. As Phil Patton has noted in an article on the turnpike's history, William Sutherland of the Pennsylvania Truck Association was an early supporter of the project, and after it opened Greyhound buses were able to cut their Pittsburgh-Harrisburg run from nine hours to five and a half.[3]

By contrast, the Merritt Parkway was rooted in the picturesque, romantic landscape

*Milford connector, Milford, bridge over the Post Road.*

tradition of Frederick Law Olmsted. True to its name, it was designed as a way through a park. The commercial traffic that was the Pennsylvania Turnpike's mainstay was completely foreign to the Merritt's conception and execution, since its underpasses and grades were built to exclude large trucks and buses.

This difference in intended use is reflected in the designs of the two routes. The sinuous curves and especially the adjustment to the topography that are the hallmarks of the Merritt were intentionally avoided on the turnpike in order to accommodate the underpowered trucks of the day. Tunnels cut through seven of the turnpike's steeper ridges, and long fills flattened other grades. And because much of the route traversed open farmland, the engineer's transit became the most important design tool: some sections as long as twelve miles were built without the slightest curve, making the highway literally recede to the horizon like a renaissance exercise in perspective drawing. The Pennsylvania Turnpike cuts across the terrain like a rail line – precisely the effect Schuyler Merritt insisted that the Fairfield County road avoid. In fact, much of the route and all of the tunnels derive from an abandoned nineteenth-century railroad scheme. In the early 1880s, the New York Central's William Vanderbilt, Andrew Carnegie, and some coinvestors undertook a plan to counter the near-monopoly of the Pennsylvania Railroad in this coal- and steel-rich area by building the competing South Pennsylvania Railroad. When the power behind the project, J. P. Morgan, saw the probable result of competition – a disastrous rate war – he and his backers pulled out, effectively killing the project. The tunnels and much of the graded right-of-way were abandoned after an investment of some $10 million and lay fallow until the proposal for a turnpike was broached in the early 1930s. With the route already mapped out and much of the initial construction already in place, it is not surprising that the Pennsylvania Turnpike was built in just twenty months and at a cost of only $60 million.[4]

The straight-arrow alignment of the turnpike may have satisfied utilitarian engineering needs, but it created unexpected problems. What curves it did have were engineered for speeds of ninety miles an hour, Patton reports, and the straightaways challenged even the most timorous driver to see what his car could do. Speed-related accidents led to the imposition of a seventy mile an hour speed limit, but for many the challenge remained. Unfortunately, the cars of the day were not up to it. Tire failures were routine, and the constant pounding at high speeds often exceeded the staying power of the cars' moving parts. I recall as a child being marooned on a postwar vacation when the

*Pennsylvania Turnpike, view
of straightaway.*

family's prewar auto burned out a wheel bearing near Somerset. The mechanic who
repaired the damage matter-of-factly allowed that it happened all the time.

If the equipment of the day was not up to the demands of the new road, neither, it
seemed, were the drivers. The long stretches of unbroken straightaway had a hypnotic
effect apparently not foreseen by the engineers who laid out the superhighway. Without
the curves and hills of the Merritt to break the monotony, many drivers were lulled into
a kind of stupor, or they became transfixed by repetitive aspects of the road – joints in
the concrete, posts along the margin – or, worse, by the vehicle immediately ahead. Like
a magnet, cars seemed drawn together, and rear-enders became as common as accidents
resulting from drivers dozing off at the wheel.

The Pennsylvania Turnpike's planners, perhaps benefiting from the experience of
the Merritt with stranded motorists, incorporated a series of service plazas along the
route, an idea pioneered on Robert Moses's parkways. These were built not in pairs
on either side of the road but singly and some distance apart, often near the exit toll
stations to discourage people from getting off the turnpike. Unlike the Merritt stations,
which were primarily intended to service the car, those on the turnpike featured what
was then a rather modest chain of restaurants and ice cream parlors run by Howard
Johnson. The most elaborate of these plazas was the colonial fieldstone South Midway
station near Bedford, which included not only a restaurant but also a motel especially
for truckers. Given the length of the turnpike, such amenities made sense. This practice

was repeated on many of the postwar interstate highways, although the restaurants have mainly given way to fast-food emporia, and the motels, privately owned, are generally built off the highway right-of-way.

The Pennsylvania Turnpike, despite its superficial similarities to the Merritt – limited access, lanes divided by landscaped medians, even Art Deco flourishes, though in the main much more restrained – is the antithesis of the parkway. It was intended for heavy through traffic, with only eleven interchanges on its entire length, whereas the Merritt was conceived as a leisure drive catering to local traffic. The designs of other highways built or started about this time show that the Merritt was thought to be the model for the future. Robert Moses's insatiable appetite for highway construction continued throughout New York State, and in California the first segment of what was to become an inhumanely complex system of "freeways" – apparently a Golden State neologism – was, like the Merritt, completed in 1940. Originally called the Arroyo Seco Parkway after the dry river valley through which it was threaded, the six-mile route is now called more prosaically the Pasadena Freeway.[5] It too was adjusted to its topography in both design and landscaping and was also characterized by narrow lanes, fairly sharp curves, and extremely tight entrances and exits. It was as if highway engineers everywhere discounted the potential speeds of the vehicles they were trying to accommodate.

The name *parkway*, if not exactly the Merritt model, was also used in such other locations as the spectacular 484-mile Blue Ridge Parkway, which runs from Virginia to North Carolina and Tennessee, connecting the Shenandoah and Great Smoky Mountains national parks. Built between 1936 and 1943, it has only two lanes and no median. The sensitivity with which this recreational highway, built by the National Park Service, was sited and landscaped is close to the spirit of the Merritt.[6] Similar concerns were put into practice in other national parkways built in the 1930s, such as those around Washington, D.C., where Gilmore Clarke served as design consultant,[7] and in the Natchez Trace Parkway, an inter-state historical drive that follows the route of an old Choctaw and Chickasaw trail, later developed by white settlers and river boatmen who used it to walk home after drifting with the current along the Ohio and Mississippi rivers down to Natchez. Another government agency, the regional Tennessee Valley Authority (TVA), also had an uncommon interest in naturalistic landscaping, a feature that marked not only the dams, for which it is best known, but also the Tennessee Valley Parkway, which wound through the area redeveloped by TVA.

Other parkways less ambitious in length sprouted in many urban areas, a byproduct of Work Projects Administration (WPA) relief programs of the 1930s.[8] Typical examples are drives through strip parks – the Oak Creek Parkway, for instance, constructed by the WPA for the Milwaukee County Park Commission – which recall Olmsted's gracious Emerald Necklace around Boston.

The George Washington Memorial Parkway, built along the Potomac River in Virginia from 1930 to 1960, and the Palisades Interstate Parkway, constructed along the Hudson River in New York and New Jersey in the 1940s, are much closer to the Merritt in spirit and design. In both cases several variations were worked on the Merritt's landscaped median. Instead of a landscaped area of constant width, these routes incorporated a variable median. This feature allowed the opposing lanes to be set at different levels to afford a view of the river to the landward traffic. It also made it possible to vary the alignment of lanes so that opposing traffic was quite invisible. Scenic overlooks were built along the Palisades Parkway for motorists to stop and take in the view of the Hudson River Valley. Another federal parkway project, the proposed Mississippi River Parkway (1949), was designed to have run through ten states from Minnesota to Louisiana, but it was never built. Too much of the route, it was decided, was already encumbered with heavy development that would have prevented the kind of naturalistic parkway the National Park Service preferred.

Parkways quickly achieved popular acclaim. Already in the 1930s the name was being applied to a number of road-building projects that had virtually nothing of the character of the Merritt. Foremost among the offenders was Robert Moses, who cyni-

*George Washington Memorial Parkway, Virginia (U.S. Department of Transportation, Federal Highway Administration).* **left**

*Arroyo Seco (now Pasadena) Freeway, Los Angeles (Department of Transportation, State of California).* **right**

cally traded on the enthusiasm that his own early parkways had generated in such exploits as the Grand Central and Cross Island parkways. More akin to interstate highways than to early parkways, they lack even the rudimentary park setting needed to justify the title. Some sections were actually elevated, so that the roadway did not make even token contact with the earth.

The Merritt Parkway's favorable reputation for its environmentally conscious design inspired a similarly sensitive approach to other matters related to the automobile. By the 1930s, the problem of where to park one's car when the destination had been reached was at least as vexing as the mess on the highways themselves. The verticalization of most United States cities through the proliferation of skyscrapers made the parking nightmare a planning concern. Using undeveloped land as surface parking lots was an inadequate solution, and the few parking garages that were built were generally ad hoc structures that hardly improved the cityscape. Some designers showed a Rube Goldberg fascination with solving the problem mechanically, as in the famous Chicago experiment that pigeonholed cars by means of elevators. More farsighted was the solution adopted by the army of architects who designed Rockefeller Center. Because the scale of the project was immense, it was quite easy to bury the parking in the bowels of the complex, hiding the sea of vehicles characteristic of surface lots. The prize for inventiveness – and the solution that best captured the spirit of the Merritt Parkway – surely goes to the architect Timothy Pflueger. His 1942 design for the Union Square garage in downtown San Francisco called for ripping up the landscaped square, building several levels of parking, then replacing the greenery and attendant civic sculpture atop the garage.[9]

Passage of the Interstate Highway Act of 1956 led to an explosion of superhighway construction. Planners had two opposing models from which to choose, the Merritt Parkway and the Pennsylvania Turnpike. For the most part, the turnpike proved to be the more compelling: its no-nonsense functionalism seemed better suited to postwar America's need to solve the urgent demands that the antiquated United States highway system be brought up to date. The vexing problem of getting heavy through traffic out of the cities was critical, and the Merritt's bucolic solution seemed at the time not to be a solution at all. Instead, the interstate highways sliced relentlessly through the cities, marooning whole neighborhoods. The urban poor would no longer live on the wrong side of the tracks, but on the wrong side of the freeway.

*Timothy Pfleuger, Union Square Garage, San Francisco (Gabriel Moulin, courtesy John Pfleuger, AIA).*

Like the Pennsylvania Turnpike, the interstate highways were designed to cover the shortest distance between two points with maximum efficiency. The Bureau of Public Roads, a federal agency, built the Washington-Baltimore Parkway in 1953, designed along the lines of the Merritt, built in a densely trafficked corridor. It was intended as a demonstration of how the interstates might be constructed. The demonstration was little noted, however, especially in the cities. Ironically, once the interstates left the urban centers, the engineers seemed in their designs to fall back on the Merritt's curving configuration to correct the mesmerizing effect of long straightaways that afflicted the Pennsylvania Turnpike.

The Merritt proved influential in its shortcomings as well as its virtues. Such design flaws as the pinched bridges, the lack of acceleration and deceleration lanes, and the tight entrance and exit ramps were all noted by highway designers, who profited from these lessons. But mainly the Merritt was admired for its successes. That thinkers as intellectually distant as Sigfried Giedion and Lewis Mumford, an International Style technocrat and a humanist with a jaundiced view of industrialization, could agree on the value of the Merritt speaks clearly of its achievement. The Merritt also spoke to advocates of regional planning and cooperation. From planning to execution, it was perhaps a more serviceable example of regionalism than the more renowned projects of the Tennessee Valley Authority because the area it covered was not so vast, nor were its goals so complex. It showed that independent governmental entities – the towns of Fairfield County, the county itself, the state, and the federal government – could set aside their own parochial interests and work successfully toward a common objective: unsnarling the traffic on the Post Road while preserving the county's natural assets.

The Merritt soon garnered kudos in such popular forums as *Life* magazine, and this widespread praise helped to make the parkway a kind of icon for planners. Unfortunately, it has more often been revered than emulated. The highways that followed the Merritt model were usually designed for recreation. New Jersey's Garden State Parkway, completed in 1956, again from designs by Gilmore Clarke, is a blend of the Pennsylvania and Merritt models. In the highly urbanized section around Newark, the road is not significantly different from the urban interstates of its generation and serves similar commuter functions. But as it swings south paralleling the New Jersey shore in its long run to Cape May, it becomes a true parkway, carrying vacationers to Atlantic City and other coastal holiday spots. There the route passes through unspoiled pine barrens with a forested median that swells to four hundred feet in some areas to retain a sense of wilderness not even imagined by the Merritt's builders. Where the opposing lanes converge to some thirty feet, a landscaped berm blocks the view of oncoming traffic and eliminates the blinding effects of approaching headlights. Picnic areas, proposed for the Merritt but never built there, are in ample supply on the Garden State. Thayer Chase's policy when designing the Merritt of rounding the tops of cuts and the bottoms of fills to avoid a man-made look as much as possible is clearly in evidence on the Garden State as well as on certain sections, especially upstate, of the New York Thruway. It also comes through on other highways where aesthetic effect was deemed as important as engineering efficiency.

Only occasionally, as in the building of the Junipero Serra Freeway – Interstate 280 south of San Francisco – has the public itself demanded that a highway through their neighborhood be designed with sensitivity to both environmental and engineering values. The sinuous curves of I-280, neatly adjusted to the topography, and the smooth organic character of its bridges and ramps make it deserving of the rather self-congratulatory title its planners gave it, "World's Most Beautiful Freeway." The Junipero

*Garden State Parkway
(Garden State Parkway).*

Serra uses differential alignments of its traffic lanes and has scenic overlooks, like the Palisades Parkway, in this case affording dramatic views of the Crystal Springs Reservoir contained in a natural fold of the earth formed by the San Andreas Fault. Interstate 280 is not called a parkway, but it is a tribute to the builders of the Merritt Parkway too seldom encountered. Although it traverses a very different landscape from the Merritt's, it reminds us of the importance of preserving the local environment and working with nature, not against it, aims that distinguish the Merritt and all the roads that followed its example.

The Merritt Parkway has collected some criticism over the years, too, especially Dunkelberger's bridge designs, which fell from favor in certain quarters. Elizabeth Mock, for example, in a book published by the Museum of Modern Art, the gatekeeper of orthodox modernism, delivered the strident opinion that the bridges used "vulgar ornament . . . peculiar to our times and easy of achievement in this docile material [concrete]."[10] Fortunately, this puritanical view has not prevailed. On the contrary, Dunkelberger's work today is esteemed, as is the parkway as a whole, precisely because it offers an antidote to the blandness of most modern highways, a blandness inspired in part by the judgments of critics like Mock.

More than fifty years after its completion, the Merritt remains a consummate design, a brilliant integration of the engineer's and the artist's crafts, a work of art that is one

*Junipero Serra Freeway near San Mateo, Calif.*

*Junipero Serra Freeway and Route 92 interchange, San Mateo, Calif.*

*Milford connector, Milford,
bridge over the Post Road.*

of the world's masterpieces of highway building. It is a convincing demonstration of
what the collaboration of inspired designers can create given sufficient freedom and
the encouragement of a determined citizenry. Perhaps the circumstances of its creation
can never be replicated – a hopeless traffic snarl that provided the need, an economic
depression that provided the means through cheap money and an army of unemployed
workers, and the chance coming together of a brilliant group of designers whose youth
and inexperience fostered experimentation and a fresh vision.

Will the Merritt Parkway, now showing its age, receive the care and attention it
deserves before it is too late? Moses and his inheritors have never been particularly rev-
erential in dealing with their parkways; the extensive changes made to sections of the
Hutchinson River Parkway, for instance, have practically remodeled the original design
out of existence. Preserving the still useful Merritt Parkway will insure the perpetua-
tion of the most beautiful and important of these 1930s experimental highways, not just
as a nostalgic bit of history, a period piece, but also as a national treasure to be used
and enjoyed and cherished.

# NOTES

## Preface

**1.** The term *limited-access*, like the highways to which it is applied, was a relatively new concept. Some planners preferred to say *controlled-access* because it avoided, they felt, the legal implication that use of a tax-supported road was somehow limited, a fear not without foundation. Legal challenges led to the adoption of clarifying legislation, first in Rhode Island in 1937, then in 1939 in Connecticut, California, and New York – *after* limited-access roads were in place in the latter states.

**2.** Sigfried Giedion, *Space, Time and Architecture*, 1st ed. (Cambridge, Mass.: Harvard University Press, 1941), p. 552.

**3.** Mumford commented on the Merritt Parkway in a lecture on urbanism at the University of California, Berkeley, in 1961. He seems not to have published those observations, but his remarks on New York's Taconic Parkway in his essay "The Highway and the City," *Architectural Record* (April 1958), could be applied as well to the Merritt. Such parkways, he wrote, "are not merely masterpieces of engineering, but consummate works of art. . . . If this standard of comeliness and beauty were kept generally in view, highway engineers would not so often lapse into the brutal assaults against the landscape and against urban order that they actually give way to when they aim solely at speed and volume of traffic" (p. 181).

## Chapter 1: Coping with the Automobile in America

**1.** Map and brochure on the Merritt Parkway published by the Bridgeport City Trust Company "as a contribution to the Centennial of Bridgeport," 1936. See also Stewart H. Holbrook, *The Old Post Road* (New York: McGraw-Hill, 1962).

**2.** Bridgeport City Trust Company brochure.

**3.** Annual report of the Fairfield County Planning Association, "Merritt Parkway Number," February 1934, p. 4. By this time 80 percent of the county's population resided in the shore towns and only 20 percent in inland towns and on farms.

**4.** U.S. Department of Transportation, *Highway Statistics Summary to 1965* (Washington, D.C., 1967), p. 23.

**5.** The first European car intended specially for the mass market was the Volkswagen, which rolled off the assembly line in 1936 (at a ceremony with Adolf Hitler in attendance) but was quickly placed on hold because of war priorities. Stephen Bayley, Philippe Garner, and Deyan Sudjic, *Twentieth Century: Style and Design* (New York: Van Nostrand Reinhold Co., 1986), pp. 144–45.

**6.** Robert Caro, *The Power Broker: Robert Moses and the Fall of New York* (New York: Random House, 1974). Moses's rise to power is treated in great detail (pp. 91–177), with special attention to his first highway schemes (pp. 161–71). A less critical biography is Joann P. Krieg, *Robert Moses: Single Minded Genius* (1987).

**7.** *New York Times*, July 10, 1990.

**8.** Gilmore D. Clarke, "The Parkway Idea," in W. Brewster Snow, ed., *The Highway and the Landscape* (New Brunswick, N.J.: Rutgers University Press, 1959), pp. 33–55. Clarke's firm, Clarke and Rapuano, in New York City, worked closely with Moses on many of his projects from the 1920s to the 1960s. They designed many parks and parkways in Westchester County and were design consultants for the New York Thruway in the 1950s.

**9.** The extensive Olmsted bibliography includes his own writings on landscape design and social issues. Recent scholarship, which has contributed to an Olmsted revival, includes Albert Fein, *Frederick Law Olmsted and the American Environmental Tradition* (New York: Braziller, 1972), and Laura Roper's excellent biography, *FLO: A Biography of Frederick Law Olmsted* (Baltimore: Johns Hopkins University Press, 1973).

**10.** The literature on the City Beautiful Movement is well summarized in Mel Scott, *American City Planning since 1890* (Berkeley and Los Angeles: University of California Press, 1969).

**11.** Moses was certainly familiar with Henry Wright's seminal study on regional planning, *Report of the Commission of Housing and Regional Planning* (Albany, N.Y., 1926), which appeared just as Moses began his ascent to power.

## Chapter 2: The Fight over a Connecticut Parkway

**1.** Fairfield County Planning Association, "Merritt Parkway Number," p. 15.

**2.** *Highway Statistics Summary to 1965*, p. 25.

**3.** The FCPA was organized under the leadership of Robert A. Crosby, the newly appointed secretary of the Bridgeport Chamber of Commerce. Crosby, a New Yorker, was an enthusiastic proponent of the regional planning ideas then current in New York State. The FCPA was headquartered in the Bridgeport Chamber of Commerce Building. *Bridgeport Post*, July 23, 1939.

**4.** *Bridgeport Post*, January 27, 1935.

**5.** *New Haven Advocate*, February 1, 1988. Merritt's comment about "a desirable element" and the FCPA's about "sharpers from out of state" veil anti-Semitism, which was more evident in restrictive real-estate covenants, exclusionary club membership policies, and similar defamatory practices directed almost exclusively at Jews.

**6.** The standard early study is John Nolen and Henry Vincent Hubbard, *Parkways and Land Values* (Cambridge, Mass.: Harvard University Press), 1937, who showed that land assessments along the Bronx River Parkway increased by 1175 percent over a twenty-year period against an average gain of 432 percent for the rest of Westchester County. See also Edward A. Sprague, "The New Highways and Property Values," pp. 147–58, and Erling D. Solberg, "Zoning for Roadside Protection," pp. 159–68, both in Snow, *Highway and the Landscape*. On the impact of the Merritt on neighboring property, see "Merritt Parkway Improves upon Dreams of Its Best Advocates," *New York Herald Tribune*, August 21, 1938.

**7.** *Stamford Advocate*, June 2, 1935.

**8.** *New Haven Advocate*, February 1, 1988. The FCPA's president, Daniel P. Sanford, was even more specific about the kind of highway the association sought: "We want to landscape it and beautify the highway so [it] won't turn out to be a mere cement belt across the County." *Bridgeport Post*, July 6, 1930. The idea of spending tax money to create "beauty" was rejected by State Senator John Lynch, Republican of West Haven: "We must be concerned here with the humble as well as the wealthy counties of the State.... If [Highway Department] plans for the beautification of the Merritt Highway do not go far enough for Fairfield County [let] the county bear the extra cost, not assess it on the State as a whole." *Bridgeport Post*, April 4, 1935.

**9.** Commissioner Cox noted, "It was ... impossible to find any route on which the opposition of land owners was not almost completely unified against encroachment." *Biennial Report of the Highway Commissioner of the State of Connecticut*, 1940, p. 129. See also Helen Binney Kitchel, "The Story of the Merritt Parkway," *Greenwich Press*, April 7, 1938. Kitchel, then a member of the state assembly, was a founding member of the FCPA.

**10.** Kitchel, "Story of the Merritt Parkway," March 24 and 31, 1938.

**11.** The Merritt was made part of the Connecticut trunk highway system by Chap. 282, Public Acts of the Legislature, 1927. *Bridgeport Post*, February 23, 1929. "Trunk highway" was a designation of the 1916 and 1921 federal highway acts under which federal funds were matched dollar for dollar with state expenditures. Only roads so designated could qualify for matching grants, however.

**12.** These rumors, never confirmed, were real enough to be discussed by Kitchel in her *Greenwich Press* history of the parkway, March 31, 1938.

**13.** *Bridgeport Post*, February 17, 1937.

**14.** MacDonald's estimates varied considerably, some running as high as $31.7 million, depending on the kind of road and its amenities. *Bridgeport Post*, March 8, 1936. By contrast, construction costs on the postwar interstate system traversing open farmland and woodland in upstate New York were about $600,000 a mile, and New Jersey's Garden State Parkway cost some $1.93 million a mile. The more urbanly sited Cross Bronx Expressway ran more than $20 million a mile – the cost of the entire Merritt – a price that includes massive graft. Joseph C. Ingraham, "Politics and Road Building," in Snow, *Highway and the Landscape*, pp. 169–81. Ingraham makes it clear that the Merritt scandal was not unique in the annals of highway construction.

**15.** The exact date of the ceremonial turning of the first shovelful of dirt is not clear. The *Bridgeport Post* reported the event in its edition of June 6, 1934, but Helen Kitchel, an eyewitness, said in her *Greenwich Press* history that it occurred on May 23. All accounts agree that First Selectman O. D. Tuthill of Greenwich manned the ceremonial shovel, that Schuyler Merritt, Wilbur Cross, and John MacDonald were in attendance, and that the site was the future bridge overpassing Riversville Road and the Byram River.

**16.** *Bridgeport Post*, May 31, 1935.

**17.** An article in the *Bridgeport Post*, November 16, 1939, summarizing the history of the parkway suggested that the bill was passed as a trade-off between Fairfield County legislators and

their Middlesex County counterparts, who wanted – and received – support for a $3 million bridge in Middletown.
**18.** *Bridgeport Post,* June 13, 1935.

### Chapter 3: Mapping the Route, Uncovering the Corruption

**1.** *Bridgeport Post,* February 23, 1929. MacDonald was craftier than his critics suspected, however. When Assemblywoman Kitchel asked him why he advocated abandoning the parkway, he responded with a smile that "he was taking this means of stirring public opinion and enlisting the necessary support. His scheme worked well." *Greenwich Press,* March 21, 1938.
**2.** The first person to use this often-invoked metaphor appears to have been Gilmore Clarke in a Hartford address reported in the *Bridgeport Post,* May 4, 1935.
**3.** *Bridgeport Post,* July 25, 1935; see also Kitchel, *Greenwich Press,* May 5, 1938.
**4.** *Bridgeport Post,* May 31, June 12, and July 5, 1935; see also Kitchel, *Greenwich Press,* May 12, 1938.
**5.** *Bridgeport Post,* April 29, 1938. Governor Cross, for his part, was supportive to the end and invited MacDonald to ride with him in the lead car of the opening ceremonies. Wilbur Cross, *Connecticut Yankee: An Autobiography* (New Haven: Yale University Press, 1943), p. 378.
**6.** The property in question was owned by the privately held Glenville Power and Water Company. Details of all properties acquired for the right-of-way, including owners, area, assessed value, and actual purchase price, are in an appendix to Robert Hurley, *Report on the State Highway Department and the Merritt Parkway,* January 6, 1938.

**7.** *Bridgeport Post,* April 29, 1938. Although the grand jury report contained more details, the Joyce story first broke in the press in a *Bridgeport Telegram* item on December 23, 1937.
**8.** *Bridgeport Post,* April 29, 1938.
**9.** *Bridgeport Post,* April 29, 1938, and Cross, *Connecticut Yankee,* p. 385.
**10.** *Bridgeport Sunday Herald,* December 19, 1937. The *Sunday Herald* rarely missed an opportunity to take a swipe at the rich. In the same issue an article naming names of recipients of Kemp's largess carried the banner headline "Who Got Slice of Cake in Land Scandal?"
**11.** *Bridgeport Sunday Herald,* December 26, 1937.
**12.** *Bridgeport Post,* December 16, 1938.

### Chapter 4: Designing and Building the Merritt Parkway

**1.** Warren M. Creamer, "The Merritt Parkway," address presented at the Fifty-second Annual Meeting, Connecticut Society of Civil Engineers, published in the society's *Fifty-second Annual Report* (1936), p. 112.
**2.** Cox, *Biennial Report* (1940), p. 130.
**3.** *Bridgeport Post,* December 14, 1934. Ironically, cyclists were prohibited on this new highway although it was the Wheelmen of America and other cycling groups, not automobile owners, who had at the turn of the century been the principal advocates of improved, hard-surfaced roads.
**4.** *Stamford Advocate,* September 2, 1990.
**5.** Unpublished letter from Wood to Helen Kitchel, October 9, 1951;. copy in Earl Wood files, Wethersfield, Conn.
**6.** On Dunkelberger's pre-Merritt work, see Gregory E. Andrews and David F. Ransom, *Structures and Styles: Guided*

*Tours of Hartford Architecture* (Hartford: Connecticut Historical Society, 1988). His personalized gothic manner can be seen, for example, in the Wethersfield Avenue Apartments (1925), p. 51.
**7.** *Bridgeport Post,* August 15, 1935.
**8.** Leslie G. Sumner, "The Bridges on the Merritt Parkway," *Engineering News Record,* September 23, 1937, p. 504.
**9.** Helen Kitchel, *Greenwich Press,* April 28, 1938.
**10.** *Bridgeport Post,* February 27, 1936.
**11.** Gebhard has written extensively on Art Deco architecture, especially in Deco-rich southern California; see David Gebhard and Harriette von Breton, *L.A. in the Thirties* (Santa Barbara and Salt Lake City: Peregrine Smith, 1975). His stylistic distinctions are noted in David Gebhard, Roger Montgomery, Robert Winter, John Woodbridge, and Sally Woodbridge, *A Guide to Architecture in San Francisco and Northern California,* 1st ed. (Santa Barbara and Salt Lake City, Peregrine Smith, 1973), pp. 541–42.
**12.** Kenneth Lynch auction catalogue, Guernsey Auctions, New York, 1985. Lynch's career as a craftsman has not been given the attention it deserves; a brief biographical note appears in the beginning of the Guernsey catalogue which marked the dispersal of Lynch's incredible stock of metal working tools and other professional property.
**13.** Leland Roth, *McKim, Mead and White, Architects* (New York: Harper and Row, 1983), pp. 257 and 405n. Roth gives the design date as 1902; McKim's first biographer and sometime partner, Charles Moore, as 1903; *The Life and Times of Charles Follen McKim* (Boston and New York: Houghton Mifflin, 1929), p. 324. Completion of the bridge was covered in both professional

and popular journals, from *Landscape Architecture*, April, 1932, to *Popular Science*, July, 1931; internationally, in Berlin, *Wasmuths Monatsheft fuer Baukunst und Staedtbau* devoted two pages to the bridge in its May, 1932, issue. The 15 low segmental arches of the bridge were meant to echo the low hills of the river site in a manner analogous to Dunkelberger's design theories.

14. George L. Dunkelberger, "Highway Architecture," address to the Fifty-eighth Annual Meeting, Connecticut Society of Civil Engineers, published in their *Fifty-eighth Annual Report* (1942), p. 112–13.

15. Pamela Allara, "The Bridges of the Merritt: Parkway Theatre," unpublished paper presented to the annual meeting of the Society for Commercial Archeology, October, 1977, p. 6; copy in Earl Wood files.

16. Dunkelberger, "Highway Architecture," p. 117.

17. Such analogies to the theater are hardly farfetched, as Rosemarie Bletter and Cervin Robinson have shown in *Skyscraper Style: Art Deco New York* (New York: Oxford University Press), 1975, where the many allusions to the theater in Art Deco design and its efforts to create a kind of make-believe world are convincingly illustrated, pp. 59–67. Dunkelberger was well versed in the Art Deco themes of the period, as many of his bridges reflect.

18. Dunkelberger, "Highway Architecture," p. 114.

19. Ibid., p. 131. The comment reflects Dunkelberger's self-effacing attitude.

20. Ibid., p. 127.

21. Earl Wood, "Development of the Merritt Parkway," *Connecticut Woodlands* 2, no. 3 (September 1937), p. 3. Covering the "scars of construction"

was discussed by Wood in a memo to MacDonald as early as October 31, 1935. Copy in Earl Wood files.

22. W. Thayer Chase, "Recollections," *New Canaan Historical Society Annual* 11, no. 1 (1990–91), p. 1.

23. Ibid.

24. *Op. cit.*, p. 6.

25. Interview with Earl Wood, July 10, 1984; see also Susan Houriet, "Engineer Nurtured Effort to Keep Merritt Parkway Green," *Stamford Advocate*, September 2, 1990.

26. Wood, "Development of the Merritt Parkway," p. 4.

27. Ibid.

28. Chase, "Recollections," p. 1.

29. Wood, "Development of the Merritt Parkway," p. 4.

30. Ibid.

31. MacDonald's meager landscaping budget was $250,000. Unpublished letter to Helen Kitchel, October 9, 1951; copy in Earl Wood files. Efforts of individuals and garden clubs to become actively involved in landscaping the parkway were repeatedly thwarted, and an FCPA-sponsored "roadside beautification" contest announced in the spring of 1934 apparently came to nothing. *Bridgeport Post*, March 28, 1934.

## Chapter 5: The Parkway's Early History and Later Development

1. Beyond the initial $400,000 federal grant that moved the Merritt bond issue through the corridors of power in Hartford, there was a promised further grant of $6.25 million and a loan of 8.5 million at 3 percent interest. In the end, the federal contribution, funneled through the WPA, amounted to well under $6 million, although the exact figure is made murky in Highway Department

documents by lumping federal funds together with state contributions. The Fairfield County bond issue of $15 million paid the bulk of the $21.5 million cost. Unpublished information sheet on the Merritt Parkway prepared by the Connecticut Highway Department, May 1946. Hoffman's "promise" of a 45 percent federal share in the project amounting to $9 million ostensibly was lost in squabbles between competing funding agencies in Washington over "man-years" of labor in the parkway's timetable. Harry Hopkins, the head of the WPA, wanted federal money spent on relief for the unemployed, not on land acquisition. *Bridgeport Telegram*, September 5, 1935. The funds may have been punitively withheld in the end after Cross, a Democrat, was defeated by the Republican Raymond Baldwin in 1938.

2. Cross, *Connecticut Yankee*, pp. 369, 379–80.

3. *Bridgeport Post*, January 7, 1938. Interest in the scandal extended well beyond Connecticut; the story of Hurley's report was picked up on the same day by the *New York Times*. The *Bridgeport Sunday Herald*, meanwhile, headlined its coverage on January 9 "Highway Cow Milked Dry," in which it detailed how favored contractors were allowed to bid low to get construction contracts and then make profits by billing the state for large cost overruns.

4. *Bridgeport Post*, January 7, 1938.

5. *Bridgeport Post*, March 1 and 3, 1938. The controversy held more than local interest: the *Hartford Courant* ran an article and its own photos on March 2, 1936.

6. Cross, *Connecticut Yankee*, p. 383; *Bridgeport Post*, March 17, 1938.

7. *Bridgeport Post*, November 14, 1937; Cross, *Connecticut Yankee*, p. 380.

8. *Bridgeport Post*, March 29, 1938; Cross, p. 387; *Bridgeport Post*, May 1, 1938.

9. *Bridgeport Post*, August 7 and 8, 1939; *Bridgeport Telegram*, January 30, 1940.

10. *Bridgeport Post*, December 18, 1937.

11. *Bridgeport Post*, January 7, 1938.

12. Cross, *Connecticut Yankee*, pp. 380, 383.

13. *Bridgeport Post*, March 9 and 14, 1937. The Yale lecture, entitled "Interurban Traffic Problems," was not Clarke's first critique of the Merritt's engineering problems. But this attack was more pointed and came at a time when rumors about Kemp's improprieties were beginning to circulate. Clarke may have been bitter over not having been hired as the Merritt's designer or at least as a consultant on the parkway's design, since his work on the Sawmill, Hutchinson River, and other New York parkways as well as the Mount Vernon and Potomac parkways near Washington had made him the country's leading authority on such designs. MacDonald's decision to keep all the design and engineering work within the Highway Department may have piqued Clarke, but it did not invalidate his criticisms.

14. *Bridgeport Post*, July 13, 1937. An aerial view of construction in progress on the Main Street interchange shows straight entrance and exit ramps. *Bridgeport Telegram*, August 1, 1938.

15. *Bridgeport Post*, January 7, 1938.

16. *New York Herald Tribune*, August 21, 1938; *Buick Magazine*, June 1938, cited in the *Bridgeport Times Star*, June 10, 1938.

17. *Bridgeport Post*, November 16,

1939; unpublished letter to William J. Cox, September 21, 1940; copy in Earl Wood files.

18. *Bridgeport Post*, June 15, 1938.

19. Ross made copies of his letter to Governor Robert Hurley available to the press. *Bridgeport Post*, June 11, 1942.

20. *Bridgeport Times Star*, September 9 and 17, 1938; *Bridgeport Telegram*, September 12, 1938; *Bridgeport Post*, September 20, 1938.

21. Cox stated that "the laws of Connecticut lay down the general principle that where a town road is connected with a state highway, the town's responsibility extends . . . to the edge of the traveled path." *Bridgeport Post*, September 11, 1939.

22. *Bridgeport Telegram*, July 2, 1938.

23. *Bridgeport Post*, July 16, 1939.

24. *Bridgeport Post*, June 7 and 14, 1939.

25. Ibid. The cost of collecting each 10 cent toll in 1939, according to Cox, was 1 cent. *Bridgeport Times Star*, January 12, 1940.

26. *Bridgeport Post*, July 24, 1939.

27. *Bridgeport Post*, June 22, 1939; *Bridgeport Telegram*, July 3, 1939.

28. *Bridgeport Post*, July 27, 1939.

29. Removal of the toll barriers on the Merritt and Wilbur Cross parkways was part of a state program to remove tolls from all state highways. The decision was made after a series of disastrous semitrailer truck crashes at toll plazas along the Connecticut Thruway (I-95) resulted in multiple fatalities. As noted, the Merritt's toll booths had been the site – or cause – of many accidents over the years, but none as deadly as those involving eighteen-wheelers on I-95.

30. *Bridgeport Post*, March 17, 1940.

31. *Bridgeport Post*, August 23, 1938.

32. Renderings for the first pair of sta-

tions in New Canaan appeared in the *Bridgeport Post*, February 28, 1939, along with notice of the commission's action.

33. Apart from Edward Ferrari's Indian and Pilgrim bas-reliefs on the Comstock Hill Road overpass in Norwalk, there is virtually nothing in Dunkelberger's other bridge designs that could be called colonial. Perhaps these colonial-style filling stations simply extend the range of his eclecticism. In his presentation "Highway Architecture" he stated: "The wooded parts of the road are enhanced by buildings designed in a rustic motif; the flat and open portions with structures laid out in a simple, colonial manner creating an atmosphere of quiet and rest" (p. 117). He did not explain why "quiet and rest" were appropriate for filling stations whereas the overpasses could be extremely animated.

34. J. B. Jackson and Ervin H. Zube, eds., *Landscapes* (1970), p. 67. On the vernacular blight most filling stations constituted in the 1920s and 1930s, see Daniel M. Bluestone, "Roadside Blight and the Reform of Commercial Architecture," in Jan Jennings, ed., *Roadside America: The Automobile in Design and Culture* (Ames: Iowa State University Press, 1990), pp. 170–84.

35. Teague was not an architect but a pioneering industrial designer whose work ranged from kitchen appliances to Pullman car interiors, X-ray machines to the Kodak folding camera;, and late in his career he designed the interiors of the Boeing 707. On his work for Texaco, see Teague, *Design This Day: The Technique of Order in the Machine Age* (New York: Harcourt Brace, 1940), fig. 111, and Charles D. Olson, "Sign of the Star: Walter Dorwin Teague and the Texas

Company," *News Journal* (Society for Commercial Archeology) 2, no. 1 (Spring 1990), pp. 1–6.

**36.** Letter from G. Albert Hill, Highway Commissioner, to James B. Lowell, Commissioner of Finance and Control, April 7, 1948, detailing the history and operations of the filling stations; copy in Earl Wood files.

**37.** The acres of grass that Earl Wood's crews planted proved so costly to maintain compared to the usual highway landscaping that the highway engineers actively worked with various lawn care product manufacturers in perfecting new types of power mowers. This eventually resulted in a 65 percent reduction in mowing costs on the Merritt and commensurate savings on similar roads elsewhere, as well as in parks around the country. It also changed domestic habits by leading to the development of manageable and efficient home lawn mowers.

**38.** Ibid.

**39.** Cox, *Biennial Report*, November 20, 1940.

**40.** *Bridgeport Post*, March 23 and 28, 1939; *Bridgeport Times Star*, March 15, 1939.

**41.** *Bridgeport Times Star*, August 10, 1940.

**42.** *Bridgeport Post*, February 17, 1942; *Bridgeport Sunday Herald*, January 25, 1942.

**43.** *Bridgeport Times Star*, December 31, 1940. This is the same Robert Hurley who had been MacDonald's nemesis.

**44.** *Bridgeport Post*, January 11, 1943; *Bridgeport Telegram*, May 28, 1943; *Bridgeport Post*, August 18, June 16, 1945.

**45.** *Bridgeport Post*, August 18, 1946.

**46.** *Bridgeport Telegram*, November 17, 1939.

**47.** *Bridgeport Post*, April 4, 1940.

**48.** *Bridgeport Telegram*, June 6, 1945; *Bridgeport Post*, January 29, 1947.

**49.** *Biennial Report* (1940), p. 127.

**50.** Typed report of the Merritt Parkway Commission, May 1956; copy in Earl Wood files.

**51.** J. B. Rae, *The Road and the Car in American Life* (Cambridge, Mass.: MIT Press, 1971), p. 27.

**52.** *Bridgeport Post*, July 16, 1947, and May 24, 1949.

**53.** The critical assault on Art Deco extended to Dunkelberger himself when the *Architectural Forum* published a stinging indictment of the Merritt bridges under the heading "Connecticut Bridgework," October 1942, p. 2, without naming Dunkelberger as architect.

**54.** *Bridgeport Sunday Herald*, November 30, 1941.

**55.** Information from a Connecticut Museum of History exhibition on Connecticut public-works achievements held in Hartford, Connecticut State Library, 1989.

**56.** Remarks by Paul Timpanelli, first selectman, Trumbull, at the Merritt Parkway Fiftieth Anniversary Forum, Trumbull Marriott Hotel, October 26, 1986. In the same period, neighboring Bridgeport experienced approximately a 9 percent decline in population but a 3 percent annual increase in traffic volume. The forum's date for the celebration is curious: two years too late to mark the ceremonial turning of the first spade of dirt, it was two years too early to commemorate the official opening festivities. The forum's sponsor, Connecticut Commuters, Inc., presumably had in mind interests other than

the preservation of the parkway in its present state.

**57.** The Highway Department hoped that the mountain laurel along the parkway would become as famous as the cherry blossoms along the Potomac in Washington. *Bridgeport Post*, August 25, 1940. Eleanor Roosevelt is reported to have driven the parkway every spring to see the laurels and dogwoods in bloom.

**58.** *New York Times*, July 9, 1991.

**59.** Karl F. Crawford, Chief Engineer, Connecticut Department of Transportation, letter to Pamela E. Allara concerning the highway 25 and 8 interchanges, June 29, 1978; copy in Earl Wood files.

**60.** Ibid.

**61.** *Connecticut Preservation News* 13, no. 5 (1990), p. 3. The lead article and several supporting items in this issue are devoted to the Merritt Parkway. Anselmo had offered a $1 million donation in 1988 to fund a preservation and restoration endowment for the parkway, an offer he withdrew after a disagreement with the DOT over removal of the toll booths, which he favored.

**62.** *Connecticut Preservation News*, p. 3.

## Chapter 6: The Merritt Parkway's Long Shadow

**1.** Christopher Tunnard and Boris Pushkarev, *Man-Made America: Chaos or Control?* (New Haven: Yale University Press, 1963), pp. 164–65. The German experiments were closely watched by American highway planners.

**2.** Bel Geddes published his ideas on transportation using many photographs of the sprawling World's Fair model in *Magic Motorways* (New York: Random House, 1940). His illustrations included the Merritt Parkway, but curiously, his caption only discusses it in terms of the added cost resulting from Kemp's graft, pp. 178–79.

**3.** Phil Patton, "A Quick Way from Here to There Was Also a Frolic," *Smithsonian* 21, no. 7 (November 1990), p. 106. The emphasis on engineering efficiency at the expense of aesthetic considerations was decried early on by Gilmore Clarke, "Pennsylvania Turnpike: Beauty a Wanting Factor in the Turnpike Design," *Landscape Architecture* 32, no. 1 (January 1942), pp. 53–54.

**4.** Patton, "Quick Way," pp. 100–102; on the railroad forbear of the turnpike, see William Shank, *Vanderbilt's Folly: A History of the Pennsylvania Turnpike* (American Canal and Transportation Center, 1973). Although expediting traffic was a consideration, building the turnpike had as much to do with relieving severe unemployment in the region. See Rae, *Road and the Car*, pp. 80–81. Massive infusions of federal money in Pennsylvania also distinguished the two projects. Pennsylvania's fast-track construction timetable appealed to WPA chief Harry Hopkins.

**5.** On the Arroyo Seco Parkway and the development of the Los Angeles freeway network, see David Brodsly, *L.A. Freeway* (Berkeley and Los Angeles: University of California Press, 1981).

**6.** The National Park Service appears to have been the major employer of landscape architects in the United States during the 1930s as a result of the Civilian Conservation Corps and other New Deal programs. Phoebe Cutler, *The Public Landscape of the New Deal* (New Haven: Yale University Press, 1985), pp. 84–85. The park service's contributions are summarized in Norman T. Newton, *Design on the Land: The Development of Landscape Architecture* (Cambridge, Mass.: Harvard University Press, 1971), pp. 530–95.

**7.** On Clarke's contributions to Washington's highway system, see Sara Amy Leach, "Fifty Years of Parkway Construction in and around the Nation's Capital," in Jennings, *Roadside America*, pp. 185–97.

**8.** Cutler, *Public Landscape*, pp. 54–55.

**9.** Pflueger's brother and associate, Milton, indicates that the Union Square project was "conceived in the mid '30s," but it underwent protracted design refinement and was not completed until 1942. See Milton T. Pflueger, *Time and Tim Remembered* (San Francisco: Pflueger Architects, 1985), p. 36.

**10.** Elizabeth Mock, *The Architecture of Bridges* (New York: Museum of Modern Art, 1949), pp. 84–85.

# INDEX